SCOTT FORESMAN · ADDISON WESLEY

Mathematics

Math Diagnosis and Intervention System

Booklet E

**Problem Solving
in Grades 1–3**

Overview of Math Diagnosis and Intervention System

The system can be used in a variety of situations:

- **During school** Use the system for intervention on prerequisite skills at the beginning of the year, the beginning of a chapter, or the beginning of a lesson. Use for intervention during the chapter when more is needed beyond the resources already provided for the lesson.

- **After-school, Saturday-school, summer-school (intersession) programs** Use the system for intervention offered in special programs. The booklets are also available as workbooks.

The system provides resources for:

- **Assessment** For each of Grades K–6, a Diagnostic Test is provided that assesses that grade. Use a test at the start of the year for entry-level assessment or anytime during the year as a summative evaluation.

- **Diagnosis** An item analysis identifies areas where intervention is needed.

- **Intervention** Booklets A–M identify specific topics and assign a number to each topic, for example, A12 or E10. For each topic, there is a page of Intervention Practice and a two-page Intervention Lesson that cover the same content taught in a lesson of the program.

- **Monitoring** The Teaching Guide provides both Individual Record Forms and Class Record Forms to monitor student progress.

Editorial Offices: Glenview, Illinois • Parsippany, New Jersey • New York, New York

Sales Offices: Parsippany, New Jersey • Duluth, Georgia • Glenview, Illinois
Coppell, Texas • Ontario, California • Mesa, Arizona

ISBN: 0-328-07648-1

Table of Contents

Table of Contents continued

Name _______________________________

Problem-Solving Skill
Use Data from a Chart

Example

How can you give an equal share of crackers to each of 4 children?

The chart shows there are 8 crackers.
Use 8 counters to represent the crackers.

Snacks		
Crackers	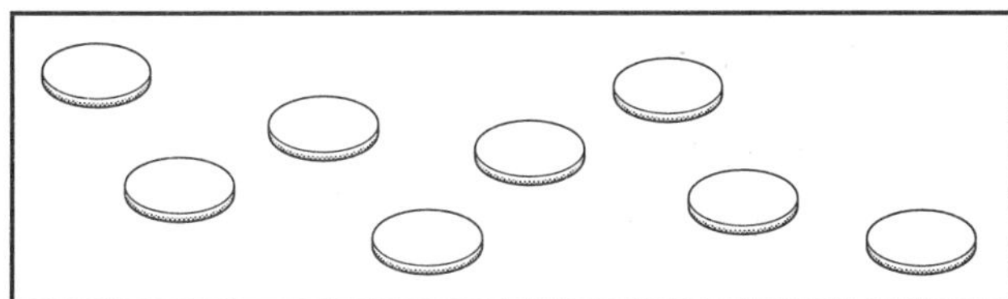	8
Apples		6
Bananas		12

First give one counter to each child.

More counters can still be used.
Give one more counter to each child.

All the counters were used.

Each child gets  crackers.

Name _______________________________

Problem-Solving Skill: Use Data from a Chart (continued)

Use the chart and counters to solve.
Draw equal shares.

1. All the apples are shared by 3 children.

Each child gets  apples.

2. All the bananas are to be shared by 4 children.

Each child gets _______ bananas.

3. **Writing in Math** Can 3 children share the crackers equally? Explain.

____

____

2

Problem-Solving Skill
Use Data from a Graph

Example

This graph shows how many stickers Jon and Luis each have.

How many stickers does Jon have?

How many stickers does Luis have?

Our Sports Stickers	
Jon	🏈 🏈 🏈 ⚽ ⚽ ⚽ ⚽ 🏀 🏀 🏀
Luis	⛑ ⛑ 🏏 🏏 🏏 🏒

Jon has ____10____ stickers.   Luis has ____6____ stickers.

Use the graph to answer Questions 1–3.

1. Who has the most stickers? ______

2. How many stickers are there altogether? ______ stickers

3. How many more stickers does Jon have than Luis?
   ______ more stickers

Name ___________________________

Problem-Solving Skill: Use Data from a Graph (continued)

Animal Card Collections		
Dog Cards	Cat Cards	Bird Cards

Use the graph to answer Questions 4–9.

4. How many bird cards are there?

_________ bird cards

5. Of which kind of card is there the most?

____

6. How many dog and cat cards are there altogether? _______ cards

7. How many cards are there in all? _______ cards in all

Writing in Math Draw a card in the graph for the animal card that you like best. Then answer Questions 8–9.

8. I like the _________ card best.

9. Now there are _________ of my favorite cards in the graph.

4

Name _______________________

Problem-Solving Skill: Use Data from a Picture

Example

James is making a pattern with shapes.

Predict: Will he make more gray circles or black circles?

more ____________ circles

Fill in the rest of the pattern.

How many gray circles?   How many black circles?

8   4

________ gray circles   ________ black circles

---

1. Jana is making a necklace with light and dark beads.
   Predict: Will the necklace have more light beads or dark beads? more ______ beads

   Color the next three beads to continue the pattern.

   How many gray beads does it have? ______ gray beads

   How many black beads does it have? ______ black beads

5

Name ___________________________________

Problem-Solving Skill: Use Data from a Picture (continued)

2. Predict: Will the scarf have more gray sections or white sections? more _________ sections

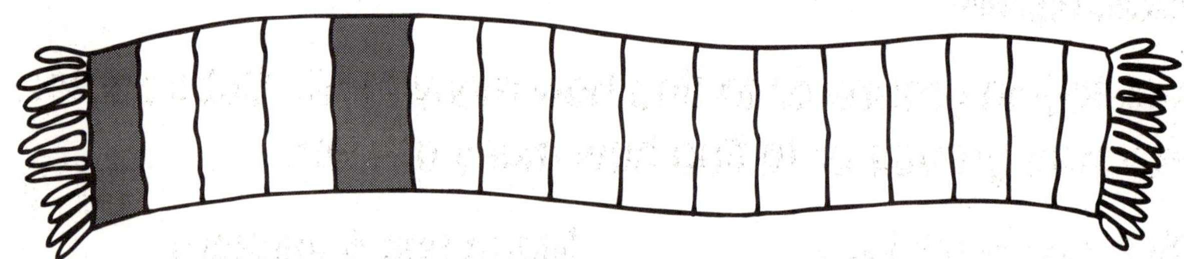

Color the sections to continue the pattern.

How many gray sections? _______ gray sections

How many white sections? _______ white sections

3. Predict: Will the table have more white tiles or gray tiles? more _________ tiles

Shade in the rest of the tiles.

How many gray tiles? _______ white tiles

How many black? _______ gray tiles

Name ____

Problem-Solving Skill
Choose an Operation

Example

Add to join groups or to find how many in all. Subtract to separate groups or to find how many are left.

Rico has 5 stickers.
He gets 2 more stickers.
How many stickers does
he have in all?

Maria has 6 stickers.
She gives 3 stickers to Dani.
How many stickers does
Maria have left?

(add)   subtract   add   (subtract)

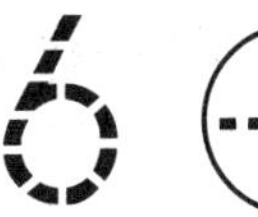   

$$5 \oplus 2 = 7 \qquad 6 \ominus 3 = 3$$

Circle **add** or **subtract**.
Then write a number sentence.

1. There are 4 frogs. 3 frogs hop away. How many frogs are left?

   add   subtract

   ___ ◯ ___ = ___

2. Leon has 7 stickers. He gets 2 more stickers. How many stickers does he have in all?

   add   subtract

   ___ ◯ ___ = ___

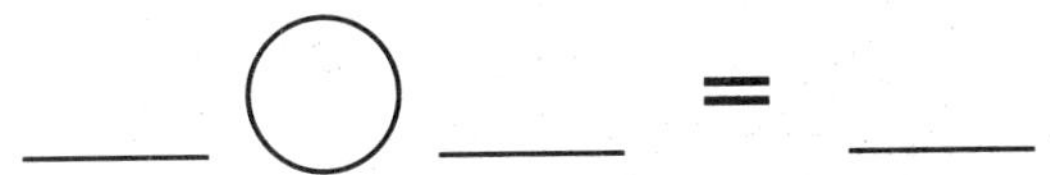

7

Problem-Solving Skill: Choose an Operation (continued)

Circle **add** or **subtract**.
Then write a number sentence.

3. 5 children are at the park.
2 children leave the park.
How many children are
left at the park?

add   subtract

___ ◯ ___ = ___

4. Jon puts 5 toys in the
box. Gil puts 4 toys in
the box. How many toys
are in the box?

add   subtract

___ ◯ ___ = ___

5. Tomas has 6 pencils. He
gives 3 away. How many
pencils does he have?

add   subtract

___ ◯ ___ = ___

6. 8 birds are in a tree.
2 birds join them. How
many birds are there
in all?

add   subtract

___ ◯ ___ = ___

7. There are 3 boys. There
are 4 girls. How many
children in all?

add   subtract

___ ◯ ___ = ___

8. There are 9 kites. 1 kite
blows away. How many
kites are left?

add   subtract

___ ◯ ___ = ___

Name ___________________________

Problem-Solving Skill: Choose an Operation

Read and Understand

Marla made 5 batches of muffins. There were 6 muffins in each batch. How many muffins did Marla make in all?

You can draw a picture to show the main idea.

Plan and Solve

The picture can also help you decide whether to add, subtract, or multiply.

You are putting together equal groups, so you should multiply.

$5 \times 6 = 30$

Marla made 30 muffins in all.

Look Back and Check

Because each batch has the same number, multiplication is the best operation to find the total.

Draw a picture to show the main idea. Use the picture to help write a number sentence and solve the problem.

1. Joan earns $5 an hour mowing lawns. She earns $3 an hour raking leaves. How much will Joan make if she mows lawns for 4 hours?

2. Carla has 16 marbles and 15 stickers. Ten of Carla's marbles are red. The rest are blue. How many blue marbles does Carla have?

Problem-Solving Skill: Choose an Operation (continued)

Draw a picture or write a number sentence to show the main idea. Then use the picture to write a number sentence and solve the problem.

Use the data in the table for Questions 3 and 4.

Number of CDs Sold	
Day	Number Sold
Thursday	6
Friday	8
Saturday	15
Sunday	11
Monday	10

3. Were more CDs sold on Thursday and Friday together, or on Saturday?

____

4. Two times as many CDs were sold on Tuesday as on Monday. How many CDs were sold on Tuesday?

____

5. Lakesha counted 20 cars that passed her house. Exactly 12 cars were white, and the rest were red. How many red cars passed Lakesha's house? _______________

6. Writing in Math Explain how you solved Question 5. Tell what operation you used.

____

____

____

Test Prep Circle the correct letter for the answer.

7. Bill has 17 baseball cards and 19 basketball cards. Which operation must you use to find the total number of cards?

A addition   **C** multiplication

B subtraction   **D** division

8. Connie feeds her dog 3 pounds of food a week. How many pounds of food does she use to feed her dog for 6 weeks?

A 9 pounds   **C** 18 pounds

B 12 pounds   **D** 24 pounds

Name ______________________________________

Problem-Solving Skill
Multiple-Step Problems

Example

Luisa has 6 colored beads.
She gets 3 more. How many
beads does she have in all?

Step 1
Add to find how many beads
Luisa has in all.

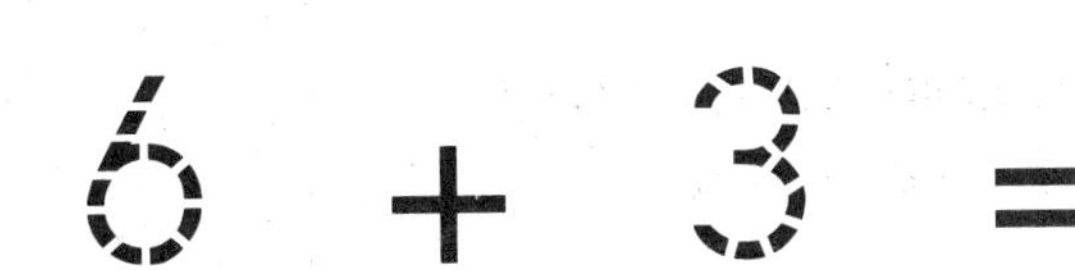

$$6 + 3 = 9 \text{ beads}$$

Luisa gives 2 beads to Maria.
How many beads does Luisa
have left?

Step 2
Subtract to find how many
beads Luisa has left.

$$9 - 2 = 7 \text{ beads left}$$

Solve each problem.

1. Kevin has 4 books. He gets 4 more books.
   How many books does he have in all?

   ____ ◯ ____ = ____ books

   Kevin gives away 3 of his books.
   How many books does he have now?

   ____ ◯ ____ = ____ books

Problem-Solving Skill: Multiple-Step Problems (continued)

Solve each problem.

2. There are 10 flowers in a vase. 6 are roses.
   The rest are lilies. How many are lilies?

   ___ ◯ ___ = ___ lilies

   Sally took out 2 lilies.
   How many lilies are left now?

   ___ ◯ ___ = ___ lilies

3. Alberto has 7 pencils in his box. He gets
   4 more. How many does he have in all?

   ___ ◯ ___ = ___ pencils

   He gives 5 pencils to Wen. How many does
   Alberto have left?

   ___ ◯ ___ = ___ pencils

4. Eva has 12 markers. She gives 5 to some friends. How
   many does she have left?

   ___ ◯ ___ = ___ markers

   Eva's teacher gives her 3 more markers. How
   many markers does Eva have now?

   ___ ◯ ___ = ___ markers

Name ________________________________

Problem-Solving Skill: Multiple-Step Problems

To solve some problems, you need to answer
hidden questions.

At the sports store, Hannah bought 2 baseballs, and Jim
bought 3 baseballs. The baseballs cost $6 each. How much
did they spend?

Read and Understand

Find how much Hannah and Jim spent altogether.

Plan and Solve

First, answer the hidden question:
How many baseballs did Hannah and Jim buy altogether? $2 + 3 = 5$

Then, solve the problem: $5 \times \$6 = \$30$

$$\begin{matrix} \text{Number of} \\ \text{baseballs Hannah} \\ \text{and Jim bought} \end{matrix} \times \begin{matrix} \text{Price of} \\ \text{a baseball} \end{matrix} = \begin{matrix} \text{Amount Hannah} \\ \text{and Jim spent} \\ \text{altogether} \end{matrix}$$

Hannah and Jim spent $30 altogether.

Write the hidden question.

1. It costs $3 to rent a video. Sue rented 4 videos, and Fran
rented 3 videos. How much did they pay in all?

____

____

2. There are 5 blank video tapes in a pack. Jamal bought
2 packs, and Bob bought 1 pack. How many blank video
tapes did they buy in all?

____

Name _______________________________________

Problem-Solving Skill: Multiple-Step Problems (continued)

Write and answer the hidden question. Then solve the problem.

Use the graph to answer Questions 3–5.

3. How many students voted for fruit or cheese?

____

____

____

Favorite Snack	
Fruit	☺ ☺ ☺
Sandwiches	☺ ☺
Cheese	☺
Pretzels	☺ ☺ ☺ ☺

Each ☺ = 3 votes.

4. How many more students voted for pretzels than voted
for sandwiches?

____

____

____

5. Number Sense If ☺ = 5 votes, how many students voted
for pretzels? _______________________

Test Prep Circle the correct letter for the answer.

6. There are 4 boxes of orange juice in a pack. There are
5 boxes of grape juice in a pack. What hidden question can
you use to find how many boxes there are in 2 orange
packs and 3 grape packs?

   A How many of each kind of juice box are there?

   B How many boxes of orange juice are in a pack?

   C How much does each pack cost?

   D How many more boxes of grape juice than orange juice
   are there?

7. Movie tickets cost $5 for adults and $2 for children under the
age of 12. How much will it cost for 3 adults and 2 children
to go to the movies?

   A $4   **B** $10   **C** $19   **D** $35

Name ___________________________________

Problem-Solving Skill: Extra Information

Example

Read the problem.
Cross out the information
you do not need.

Omar has 5 red toy cars.
~~He has 4 books.~~
He has 3 blue toy cars.
How many cars does Omar have?

> The **extra information** is the information not related to the main idea of the problem.

 +  = 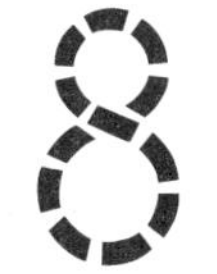 cars

---

Cross out the extra information.
Then write a number sentence to solve the problem.

1. 6 turtles are sitting in the sun.
   5 turtles are swimming in the pond.
   There are 3 lily pads in the pond.
   How many turtles are there in all?

 +  = ____ turtles

Name ____

Problem-Solving Skill: Extra Information (continued)

Cross out the extra information.
Solve the problem.

2. The library is 3 blocks from June's house. June got 5 books on Monday. She got 4 books on Saturday. How many books did she get in all?

___ + ___ = ___ books

3. Buddy has 5 markers on his desk. His friend gives him 3 more markers. He has 6 pencils inside his desk. How many markers does he have in in all?

___ + ___ = ___ markers

4. Sandi found 3 starfish at the beach. Ira found 2 pails in the sand. Ari found 6 starfish. How many starfish did they find in all?

___ + ___ = ___ starfish

5. 8 books are on a shelf. 2 books are on a table. 5 pictures are on the wall. How many books are there in all?

___ + ___ = ___ books

Name _______________________________________

Problem-Solving Skill
Extra or Missing Information

Example

Sally's painting is 14 inches long and 12 inches wide. Julie's
painting is 16 inches long. How much longer is Julie's painting
than Sally's painting?

Read and Understand

What do you know?
Sally's painting is 14 inches long. Sally's painting is 12 inches wide.
Julie's painting is 16 inches long.

What do you need to find?
I need to find how much longer one painting is than the other.

Is there any extra or missing information?
Yes, I don't need to know how wide Sally's painting is.

Plan and Solve

To find the difference between the lengths, I need to subtract.
$16 - 14 = 2$

Julie's painting is 2 inches longer than Sally's painting.

Write the extra or missing information. Solve the problem if
enough information is given.

1. Jason bought a red sweater and a black sweater.
His change was $5. How much did Jason pay for
both sweaters?

____

____

Problem-Solving Skill: Extra or Missing Information (continued)

Write the extra or missing information. Solve the problem if enough information is given.

Use the graph for Questions 2–3.

2. Turtles received 4 fewer votes than cats and 2 more votes than rabbits. How many votes did turtles receive?

____

____

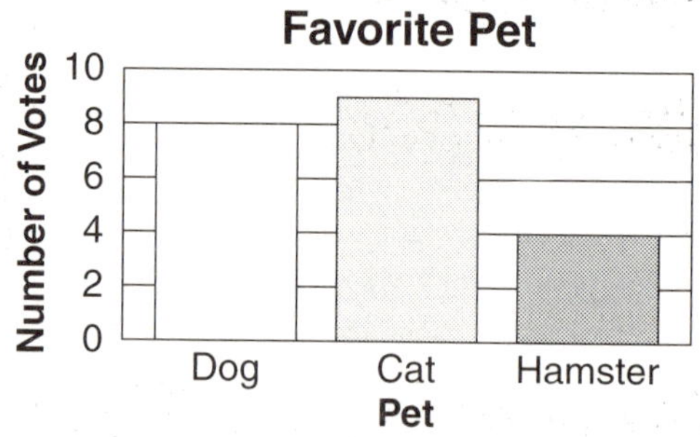

3. How many more students voted for dogs than horses?

____

____

4. Writing in Math Rose's painting is 12 inches long. Will it fit in a frame that has length of 12 inches and a width of 8 inches? Explain.

____

Test Prep Circle the correct letter for the answer.

5. Bill has 23 baseball cards, 12 basketball cards, and 4 soccer cards. Each card cost $1.00. What extra information is not needed to find how many cards Bill has in all?

  A Bill has 23 baseball cards.   **C** Bill has 4 soccer cards.

  B Bill has 12 basketball cards.   **D** Each card cost $1.00.

6. Harold placed 3 pieces of string end-to-end on his desk. The first piece is 16 inches long and the second is 8 inches long. What information do you need to find the total length of the 3 pieces of string?

  A the length of the first piece   **C** the length of the second piece

  B the length of the third piece   **D** the length of Harold's desk

18

Name ___________________________________

Problem-Solving Skill
Exact Answer or Estimate?

Example 1

Jim has 30¢.

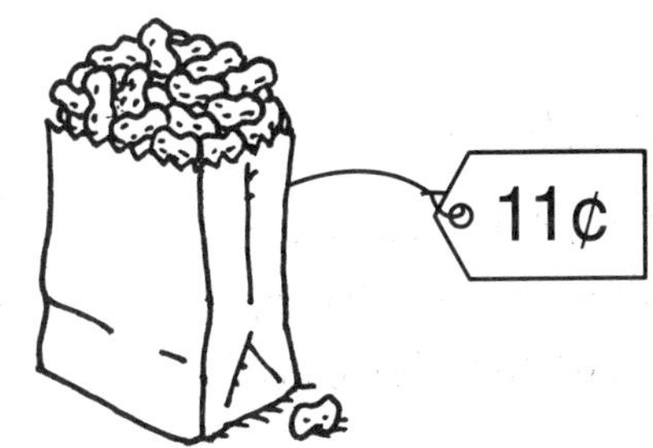

He wants to buy 2 bags of peanuts.

Does he have enough money to buy the peanuts?

Read and Understand

You need to know if 2 bags of peanuts are less than 30¢.

Do you need an exact answer or an estimate?

Plan and Solve

1 bag of peanuts costs about 10¢, so 2 bags of peanuts will cost about 20¢.

You can estimate that 30¢ is enough to buy 2 bags of peanuts.

exact answer   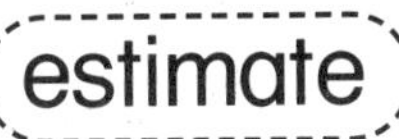

Look Back and Check

Does your answer make sense?

Problem-Solving Skill: Exact Answer or Estimate? (continued)

Is an exact answer or an estimate needed to solve
the problem.

Circle **exact answer** or **estimate.**

1. Meg is having a party with 10 friends.
   She has 2 bags of balloons.
   There are 6 balloons in a bag.
   Does she have enough balloons for all of the children?

   exact answer   estimate

---

2. Jon wants to buy a pencil that costs 6¢. Jon has a dime.
   How much change will he get?

   exact answer   estimate

---

3. There are 5 party hats in a package.
   Shawon buys 3 packages.
   Are there enough hats for 20 children?

   exact answer   estimate

---

4. David wants to buy 2 boxes of toy cars.
   There are 9 cars in each box.
   How many cars will David have?

   exact answer   estimate

Name _______________________________

Problem-Solving Skill: Exact or Estimate?

Example

Class 1 collected 295 cans. Class 2 collected 123 cans. Class 3 collected 205 cans. Did the classes collect at least 500 cans?

Read and Understand

Tell what you are trying to find: Did the classes collect at least 500 cans?

Decide if an estimate is enough. Yes, you can compare an estimate to 500 cans.

Plan and Solve

Make an organized list.

295 is about 300.
123 is about 100.
215 is about 200.

Add $300 + 100 + 200 = 600$
Compare   600 is greater than 500.

The students collected more than 500 cans.

For Questions 1–3, use the Sticker problem.

> **Stickers** Tina had 282 stickers. She bought 218 more, and then she got 125 stickers for her birthday. Pat has 875 stickers. Who has more stickers?

1. What do you know, and what are you trying to find?

____

____

2. Is an estimate enough?

____

3. Solve the problem.

____

Name _______________________________________

Problem-Solving Skill: Exact or Estimate? (continued)

For Questions 4–6, use the Soccer Game problem.

4. What do you know, and what are you trying to find?

____

____

____

____

> An indoor arena seats 920 people to watch a soccer game. So far, 794 people are seated to watch the soccer game. Can 115 more people be seated in the arena? Explain.

5. Is an estimate enough?

____

____

6. Solve the problem. Give your answer in a complete sentence.

____

____

Test Prep Circle the correct letter for the answer.

7. Which question can you answer by estimating? Fred has 275 stamps. Marcos has 391 stamps.

A How many stamps do they have in all?

B How many more stamps than Fred does Marcos have?

C Do they have at least 800 stamps in all?

D How many fewer stamps than Marcos does Fred have?

Name ____

Problem-Solving Skill: Read and Understand

Example

Karen had some stickers. She gave 4 butterfly stickers and 5 flag stickers to Bill. How many stickers did Karen give to Bill?

Read and Understand

What do you know? Karen gave Bill 4 butterfly stickers and 5 flag stickers.

What are you trying to find? The total number of stickers Karen gave to Bill.

4 butterfly stickers	5 flag stickers
Total number of stickers	

Plan and Solve

Use addition to find the answer. $4 + 5 = 9$ stickers

Karen gave Bill 9 stickers.

Look Back and Check

Using addition is okay because you need to put together two kinds of stickers.

Solve the problem. Write the answer in a complete sentence.

1. Harold collects stamps. He has 30 stamps from the United States and 20 stamps from other countries. How many more United States stamps does Harold have than foreign stamps?

____

____

Name ____

Problem-Solving Skill: Read and Understand (continued)

Solve each problem. Write the answer in a complete sentence.

2. Some fourth-grade students took a survey about cats and dogs. They found that 7 students like cats the best and 11 students like dogs the best. How many students voted for their favorite pet?

____

____

3. Jared ran 2 miles on Monday, 4 miles on Tuesday, and 6 miles on Wednesday. If Jared continued to increase his running by this pattern, how many miles did he run on Thursday?

____

____

4. Brittany had 3 pizzas. She cut 1 pizza into 8 slices and 2 pizzas into 6 slices. How many slices of pizza did Brittany have?

____

____

5. Writing in Math Explain how you found the answer to Question 4.

____

____

Test Prep Circle the correct letter for the answer.

6. Ed counted the fish in his tank. He counted 7 large goldfish and 3 small goldfish. He counted 2 large angelfish and 5 small angelfish. How many large fish are in Ed's tank?

A 8 large fish   **C** 10 large fish

B 9 large fish   **D** 17 large fish

Name _______________________

Problem-Solving Skill: Plan and Solve

Example

You can use these steps to plan and solve a problem.

On Day 1, Ti gets 1 dime. Each day she doubles the number of dimes she gets. How much money will Ti have after 4 days?

Plan and Solve

Step 1: Choose a Strategy
- Draw a picture.
- Make an organized list.
- Make a table.
- Make a graph.
- Act it out/use objects.
- Look for a pattern.
- Try, check, and revise.
- Write a number sentence.
- Use logical reasoning.
- Solve a simpler problem.
- Work backward.

Step 2: Stuck? Don't give up. Try these.
- Reread the problem.
- Tell the problem in your own words.
- Tell what you know.
- Identify key facts and details.
- Show the main idea.
- Try a different strategy.
- Retrace your steps.

Step 3: Answer the question in the problem.
What strategy can be used? A table can make the problem easier.

Day	Dimes
1	1 dime
2	2 dimes
3	4 dimes
4	8 dimes

$1 + 2 + 4 + 8 = 15$

Answer the problem: Ti will have 15 dimes, or $1.50, after 4 days.

Ti's garden is a rectangle, 6 feet long and 4 feet wide. Ti wants to put stakes 1 foot apart around the edge of the garden. How many stakes does Ti need?

1. Solve the problem. Write the answer in a complete sentence.

____

Name ______________________________

Problem-Solving Skill: Plan and Solve (continued)

Solve each problem. Write the answer in a complete sentence.

2. When playing soccer, Sue can wear a red shirt or a white
shirt. She can wear black shorts or red shorts. How many
different soccer uniforms are possible?

____

3. Carlos made a pattern out of shapes. He used a red
hexagon, then two yellow triangles, then three blue circles,
a red hexagon, then two yellow triangles, then three blue
circles, and so on, until he used 12 blue circles. How many
shapes did he use in all?

____

4. It costs 25¢ to park for 1 hour. The parking meter can take
any combinations of quarters, dimes, and nickels. How
many ways can you put 25¢ in this parking meter?

____

5. Writing in Math For the Parking Meter problem, tell what
you know and what you are trying to find.

____

____

Test Prep Circle the correct letter for the answer.

6. Which two numbers have a sum of 10 and a difference of 2?

    A 9 and 1   **B** 5 and 5   **C** 7 and 3   **D** 6 and 4

Name _______________________

Problem-Solving Skill
Look Back and Check

Example

Trish has 6 flowers.
She gives 2 flowers to her friend.
How many flowers does she have left?

Think: $6 - 2 = 4$ flowers

Does the answer make sense?

She gave flowers away.
4 flowers is **less** than 6 flowers.
Look back and check.

$6 - 2 = 4$

Solve each problem.
Write **more** or **less** to check your answers.

1. Julio had 7 fish.
   He purchased 3 more.
   How many fish does he have? _________ fish

   Does Julio have **more** or **less** than 7 fish? _________

2. Zoe gave gifts to 3 friends
   She gave 2 gifts to each friend.
   How many gifts did she give? _________ gifts

   Did Zoe give **more** or **less** than 2 gifts? _________

27

Problem-Solving Skill: Look Back and Check (continued)

Solve each problem.
Write **more** or **less** to check your answers.

3. Tilly had 17 cups of lemonade.

    Tilly sold 8 cups.

    How many cups does Tilly have left? _________ cups

    Does Tilly have **more** or **less** than 17 cups left? _________

4. Zach ran 2 miles.

    Then he ran 3 more miles.

    How far did he run? _________ miles

    Did Zach run **more** or **less** than 3 miles? _________

5. Susan built 12 birdhouses.

    She sold 3 birdhouses.

    How many birdhouses does she have?

    _________ birdhouses

    Does Susan have **more** or **less** than 12 birdhouses?

    ____

6. Hira has 5 fish and 2 dogs.

    How many pets does Hira have? _________ pets.

    Does Hira have **more** or **less** than 5 pets? _________

Name _______________________________________

Problem-Solving Skill: Look Back and Check

Example

You are not finished with a problem until you look back and check your answer.

Jeff bought a total of 5 seed packets. Jeff bought 2 packets of flower seeds for $2 each and 3 packets of vegetable seeds for $3 each. What is the total cost of the seed packets that Jeff bought?

$2 + $2 + $3 + $3 + $3 = $13

Look Back and Check

Step 1: Check your answer. Yes, I did find the total cost of the seed packets.

Step 2: Check your work. The answer is reasonable. Two packets at $2 each is $4. Three packets at $3 each is $9. $4 + $9 = $13. Addition is the right operation to find a total cost of buying many items.

Kerri solved the Buying Seeds problem by writing the number sentence $2 + $3 = $5. She said the total cost of the packets was $5. Look back and check Kerri's work.

1. Did Kerri answer the right question?

____

____

2. Is Kerri's work correct? Explain.

____

____

____

Name _______________________________

Problem-Solving Skill: Look Back and Check (continued)

Solve each problem. Write the answer in a complete sentence.
Look back and check your work.

3. You get 2 free pencils for each notebook you buy at The
School Supply Store. How many free pencils would you get
if you bought 4 notebooks?

____

____

4. Fran has 30 large shells and 10 small shells. Alan has
40 large shells and 20 small shells. Who has more shells?

____

____

5. Writing in Math Choose Question 3 or 4. Tell what
strategy you used to solve the problem and explain how
you solved it. How did you check that your answer makes
sense?

____

____

____

Test Prep Circle the correct letter for the answer.

6. Each of the three shelves have one pair of shoes on them.
The colors of the shoes are brown, black, and white. The
brown shoes are on the middle shelf. The black shoes are
not on the top shelf. On which shelf are the white shoes?

A top shelf   **C** bottom shelf

B middle shelf   **D** top and middle shelves

Name ____

Problem-Solving Skill
Translating Words to Expressions

Example

Translating words to a numerical expression can help you solve
a problem.

There are 17 Asian elephants and 12
African elephants in the zoo. Write a
numerical expression that shows the
total number of elephants in the zoo.

The words in the problem give you
clues about the operation.

Word or Phrase	Use
Sum; total; increase; together; plus	+
Difference; less than; decrease; minus	−
Product; times; double; twice	×
Quotient; equal groups; shared equally	÷

Read and Understand

There are 17 Asian elephants in the zoo.
There are 12 African elephants in the zoo.

Plan and Solve

Translate words into expressions.

Think: Total of 17 Asian elephants and 12 African elephants
Write: 17 + 12

Look Back and Check

The numerical expression 17 + 12 shows that 12 more than
17 is the total number of elephants in the zoo.

Write the numerical expression for each word phrase.

1. 2 times as many as 4 marbles   _______________

2. The total of 13 cats and 7 dogs   _______________

3. $35 decreased by $5   _______________

Name ______________________________

Problem-Solving Skill
Translating Words to Expressions (continued)

Write the numerical expression for each word phrase.

4. 12 pennies shared equally by 3 people _______________

5. 25 baseballs minus 3 baseballs _______________

6. The sum of 11 and 24 _______________

7. 3 times as many as 2 apples _______________

8. 5 increased by 2 _______________

9. 18 less than 30 minutes _______________

10. 10 students separated into 2 equal groups _______________

11. Reasoning If you have 3 fewer quarters than
dimes, do you have 3 more dimes than quarters? _______________

Test Prep Which expression matches each word phrase?
Circle the correct letter for the answer.

12. $12 less than $20

    A $12 + $20   **C** $12 − $20

    B $20 − $12   **D** $20 × $12

13. 6 groups of birds with 2 birds in each group

    A 6 + 2   **B** 6 − 2   **C** 2 × 6   **D** 6 ÷ 2

Problem-Solving Skill: Writing to Explain

Example

You can write to explain an estimate by telling the steps you used.

CDs cost $11 each. DVDs cost $19 each. Do you need more than $20 to buy both a CD and a DVD? Explain how you made your estimate.

Writing a Math Explanation

Write your estimate.	You would need more than $20.
Write your explanation in steps.	Step 1: I rounded $11 to $10 and $19 to $20. I estimated the cost of buying a CD and a DVD: $10 + $20 = $30
	Step 2: $30 is more than $20.

Write to explain.

1. Sliced turkey costs $2.89 per pound. Sliced beef costs $3.11 per pound. Marjorie buys 2 pounds of turkey and 1 pound of beef. If she pays for the meat with a $10 bill, will she get change? Explain how you made your estimate.

____

____

____

Name ____

Problem-Solving Skill: Writing to Explain (continued)

Write to explain.

2. Explain how the number of eggs changes as the number of dozens changes.

Dozens	1	2	3	4	5
Eggs	12	24	36	48	60

____

____

3. A jar of beans is one-third full. There are 47 beans in the jar now. About how many beans would fill the jar? Explain how you made your estimate.

____

____

____

4. Reasoning Explain why you can estimate to solve Question 3.

____

____

Test Prep Circle the correct letter for the answer.

5. Ramon read 92 pages of a book. Stella read 183 pages of a different book.

   A Stella read about 100 more pages than Ramon.

   B Ramon read about 100 more pages than Stella.

   C Stella read about 10 pages more than Ramon.

   D Ramon read about 10 pages more than Stella.

Name ________________________________

Problem-Solving Strategy: Writing to Compare

Example

You can write to compare by looking closely at the data.

The practice schedules for two basketball teams are shown below.

Basketball Practice			
	Start Time	**Water Break**	**End Time**
Team 1	3:00 P.M.	3:50 P.M.	4:00 P.M.
Team 2	4:00 P.M.	4:45 P.M.	5:15 P.M.

Write two statements that compare the data in the schedule.

Writing a Math Comparison

Look closely at the data.
How are the data alike?
How are they different?

Team 1 starts practice 1 hour earlier than Team 2.

Use words such as "most," "more," and "about the same."

Team 2 has more time for a water break than Team 1 has.

Write to compare.

1. What other comparison statement can you make about the data in the schedule?

____

____

2. What comparison words did you use to answer Question 1?

____

Name _______________________________

Problem-Solving Strategy: Writing to Compare (continued)

Write to compare.

3. Use the pictographs below. Write two statements that compare the data on the graphs.

Favorite Snacks of Ms. Low's Class	
Cheese	★ ★ ★
Chips	★ ⌐
Fruit	★ ★ ★ ★
Pretzels	★ ★ ★ ★ ★

Each ★ = 2 votes

Favorite Snacks of Mr. Tan's Class	
Cheese	★ ★ ★
Chips	★
Fruit	★ ★ ⌐
Pretzels	★ ★ ★ ★ ★ ★

Each ★ = 2 votes

____

____

____

____

Test Prep Circle the correct letter for the answer.

4. Use the bar graphs below. Which comparison statement is true?

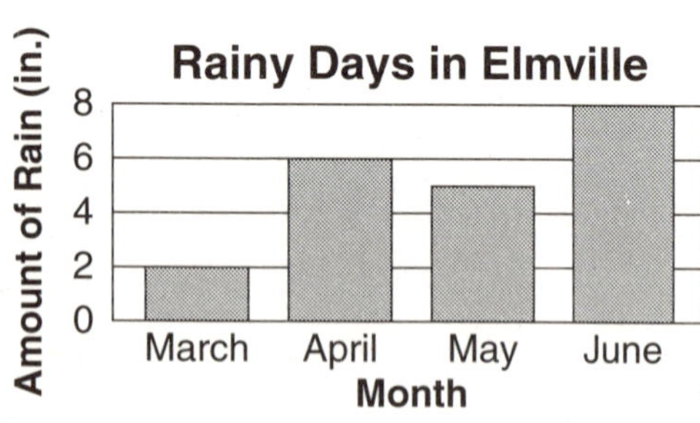

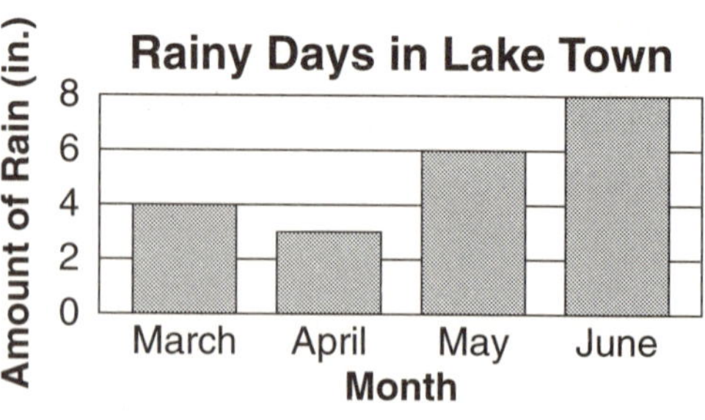

A It rained more in Elmville in March than it did in Lake Town.

B It rained more in Lake Town in April than it did in Elmville.

C It rained less in Elmville in May than it did in Lake Town.

D It rained less in Lake Town in June than it did in Elmville.

Name _______________________

Problem Solving Strategy: Writing to Describe

Example

You can write to describe geometric figures by using geometric terms such as *side, edge, face, corner,* and *surface.*

Solid Figures Descriptions of solid figures may mention the number of edges and corners, the number and shape of the faces, whether there are curved surfaces, and whether the solid has the ability to roll.

Use geometric terms to describe how the rectangular prism and the cube are alike.

Writing a Math Description

The rectangular prism and the cube both have six faces, twelve edges, and eight corners. They both have all flat surfaces. Neither of them rolls. These two figures are different because the faces of a rectangular prism are not all squares like the faces of a cube.

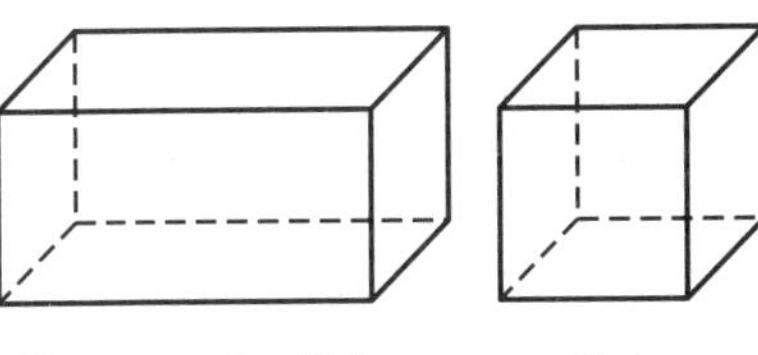

Rectangular Prism   Cube

Write to describe.

1. Write a statement that describes how the figures at the right are alike.

____

____

____

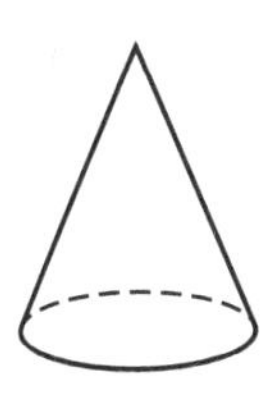
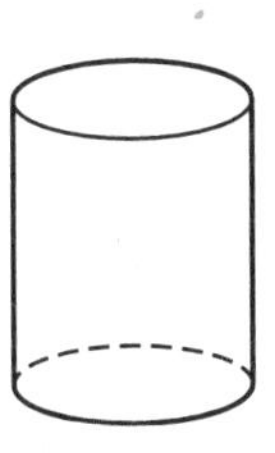

Cone   Cylinder

37

Name _______________________

Problem Solving Strategy: Writing to Describe (continued)

Write to describe.

2. Write a statement that describes how the box of cereal and the can of soup are different.

____

____

3. Write a statement that describes how the hexagon and the square are alike.

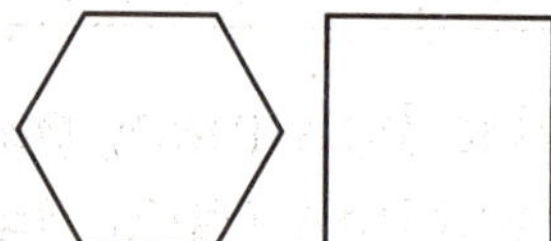

____

____

____

4. Write a statement that describes how the hexagon and the square are different.

____

____

5. Reasoning I am a solid figure with six faces, twelve edges, and eight corners. I am not a rectangular prism. What kind of solid figure am I? _______________________

Test Prep Circle the correct letter for the answer.

6. Use the figures to the right. Which description is true?

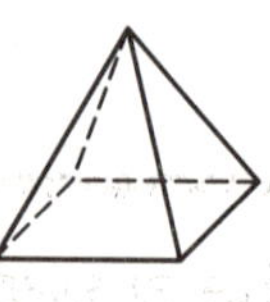
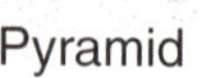
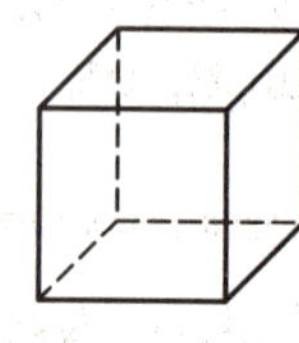

A The pyramid and cube both have eight corners.

B The pyramid has five faces, but the cube has six faces.

C The pyramid and cube can both roll.

D The pyramid and cube both have twelve edges.

Pyramid   Cube

38

Name ______________________________

Problem-Solving Skill
Interpreting Remainders

Example

George has 58 pictures to put in a photo album. Each page in the album will hold 8 pictures. If he fills each page before starting a new page, how many photos will be on the last page?

Read and Understand

Find how many pages will be used.
Find how many pages will be filled completely.
Find how many pictures are on a page that is not completely filled.

Plan and Solve

Divide to find the answer: $58 \div 8 = 7 \text{ R}2$
8 pages will be used. 7 pages will be completely filled.
The remainder tells us that there are 2 pictures on the page that is **not** filled.

Look Back and Check

With 8 photos on each page, seven pages will be filled with 56 photos ($7 \times 8 = 56$). One more page is needed to hold the remaining 2 pictures. So, 8 pages will be used to hold the pictures.

Solve. Write the answer in a complete sentence.

1. There are 27 students going to a museum. Each van can hold 6 students. How many vans will be needed?

____

Name _______________________________

Problem-Solving Skill: Interpreting Remainders (continued)

Solve. Write the answer in a complete sentence.

2. Ed is making stuffed animals. He needs 2 buttons to use as
eyes for each animal. If Ed has 15 buttons, how many
stuffed animals can he make? How many buttons are left
over?

____

3. Ms. Ramirez is putting 25 fourth-graders into teams of 6
students each. How many teams can she make? How many
students are not on a team?

____

4. Juanita is knitting socks. Each pair of socks needs 3 balls of
yarn. She has 20 balls of yarn. How many balls of yarn will
not be used?

____

5. Writing in Math Write a story problem that can be solved
using $23 \div 5 = 4 \text{ R}3$. Write and explain what the
remainder means in your story problem.

____

____

____

Test Prep   Circle the correct letter for the answer.

6. Sue has a rock collection. The rocks are stored in cases
that each hold 8 rocks. She has 50 rocks. How many cases
of rocks does Sue need for her collection?

A 8 cases   **B** 7 cases   **C** 6 cases   **D** 5 cases

40

Name ___________________________________

Problem-Solving Strategy
Draw a Picture

Example

Tom has 5 baseball cards.
Miguel has 4 baseball cards.
How many cards do they
have in all?

Tom's cards   Miguel's cards

Read and Understand

You need to find how many cards there are in all.

Plan and Solve

Draw a picture.
Then write a number sentence. $\underline{5} + \underline{4} = \underline{9}$ cards

Look Back and Check

How can you be sure your answer is correct?

Draw a picture.
Then write a number sentence.

Rena's cards   Kathy's cards

1. Rena has 3 sports cards.
   Kathy has 7 sports cards.
   How many cards do they have in all?

   ____ + ____ = ____ cards

Name ___________________________

Problem-Solving Strategy: Draw a Picture (continued)

Draw a picture.
Then write a number sentence.

2. Bonnie has 4 markers.
    Ravi has 3 markers.
    How many markers do they have in all?

    ____ + ____ = ____ markers

---

3. Roberto has 8 baseballs.
    Daniel has 3 baseballs.
    How many baseballs do they have in all?

    ____ + ____ = ____ baseballs

---

4. Lisa has 4 flowers.
    Elisa has 5 flowers.
    How many flowers do they have in all?

    ____ + ____ = ____ flowers

Name ___________________________________

Problem-Solving Strategy: Draw a Picture

Example

Mr. George is putting a fence along the back of his yard. The
wooden fence will be 64 feet long. There will be a post every
8 feet and a post on each end. How many posts will there be?

Read and Understand

What do you know? The fence will be 64 feet long with a post
every 8 feet and one on each end.

What are you trying to find? The number of posts Mr. George
will need for his fence.

Plan and Solve

What strategy will you use to solve the problem?
Draw a picture to represent the situation and interpret the
picture to answer the question.

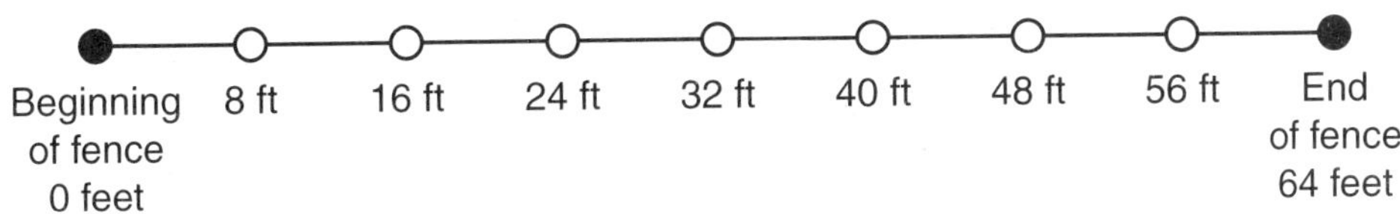

Mr. George will need 9 posts for the fence.

Look Back and Check

Step 4: Is your answer reasonable? Yes, all the posts are shown.

Solve each problem. Write the answer in a complete sentence.

1. Gail has a board 15 feet long and wants to cut it into
5 equal pieces, how many cuts will she need to make?

____

Name _______________________________

Problem-Solving Strategy: Draw a Picture (continued)

Solve each problem. Write the answer in a complete sentence.

2. The cafeteria offers a turkey or ham sandwich on whole wheat, rye or white bread. How many choices of sandwiches are there?

____

3. You are planting pepper plants in a garden. Your garden is only 48 inches long. The plants must be planted 6 inches apart and the first and last plant must be 6 inches from the edge of the garden. How many plants can you plant in a row?

____

4. Amy was third in line. Kevin was behind Gina. Meg was behind Amy. If Gina was first, who was second?

____

5. When a ball bounces, it returns to $\frac{1}{2}$ of its previous height.

If Ken drops a ball from 20 feet, how many feet will it have traveled when it hits the ground the second time?

____

6. Mollie is taller than Kristin and shorter than Mike. Ted is shorter than Mollie but taller than Kristin. Who is the tallest?

____

Test Prep Circle the correct letter for the answer.

7. Jeff gives himself 4 stamps for each stamp he gives Jack. If Jack has 5 stamps, how many does Jeff have?

A 5   **B** 8   **C** 16   **D** 20

44

Name ______________________________

Problem-Solving Strategy
Make an Organized List

Example

Find 3 ways you can make this shape using pattern blocks.

Read and Understand

You need to find all the ways that pattern blocks can make
the shape.

Plan and Solve

Make a list to help you keep track.

Ways to Make			
Shapes I used	(trapezoid)	(rhombus)	(triangle)
Way 1	1	0	1
Way 2	0	2	0
Way 3	0	0	4

Look Back and Check

Did you find 3 ways? How do you know?

45

Problem-Solving Strategy: Make an Organized List (continued)

I.   Use pattern blocks. How many ways can you make this shape? Record the blocks you used.

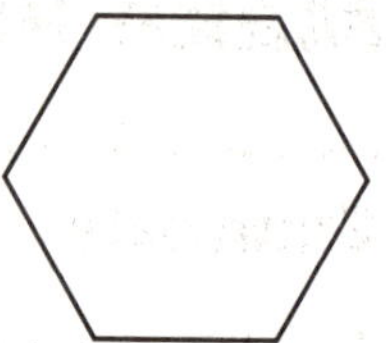

Shapes I used	Ways to Make			
Way 1	i	0	0	0
Way 2	0			
Way 3	0			
Way 4	0			
Way 5	0			
Way 6	0			
Way 7	0			
Way 8	0			

How many ways can you make a hexagon? ______________

Name ___________________________

Problem-Solving Strategy
Make an Organized List

Example

Terri has homework in English, Reading, Math, and Science. She plans to do Math first. In how many different ways can she arrange the order of her homework?

Read and Understand

What do you know? There is homework in English, Reading, Math, and Science. Math will be done first.

What are you trying to find? Find how many different ways Terri can arrange her homework.

Plan and Solve

What strategy will you use to solve the problem? Make an organized list with Math listed first.

Math, English, Reading, Science
Math, English, Science, Reading
Math, Reading, English, Science
Math, Reading, Science, English
Math, Science, English, Reading
Math, Science, Reading, English

There are six different ways.

Look Back and Check

Is your answer reasonable? Yes, Math is first and the order is different for each way.

---

1. Max, June, and Greg are posing for a picture. If they stand in one row, how many different ways can they pose?

____

Name _______________________________________

Problem-Solving Strategy
Make an Organized List (continued)

Solve each problem.

2. At a jewelry store, you can have your purchase gift-wrapped in silver, gold, or red paper with a white, pink, or blue ribbon. You can choose one color of paper and one color of ribbon. How many gift-wrap combinations are available?

____

3. Mr. Johnson is making sandwiches. He has wheat bread and rye bread. He has ham and salami. He also has colby and cheddar cheese. Each sandwich will have one kind of bread, one kind of meat, and one kind of cheese. How many different kinds of sandwiches can he make?

____

4. Leslie has a penny, a nickel, and a dime in her pocket. If she picks out 2 coins, what amounts of money could she get?

____

5. Each child at Heather's party has chosen a sandwich and a drink. If there are 7 children at the party, can they each have a different lunch?

Sandwiches	Drinks
Turkey	Milk
Ham	Juice
Tuna	
Peanut butter	

Test Prep Circle the correct letter for the answer.

6. Paul, Steve, and Bridget get on an elevator. The boys want to be polite and let Bridget go first. In how many different ways can they arrange their order to get on the elevator?

A 1 **B** 2 **C** 3 **D** 9

Name ______________________________

Problem-Solving Strategy
Make a Table

Example

Carlos has a basketball,
a baseball, and a soccer ball.

He wants to put the balls in
boxes. He has 2 boxes. How
many different ways can he
put the 3 balls in the boxes?

Read and Understand

You need to find how many different ways Carlos can put the
balls in the boxes.

Plan and Solve

You can make a table. Then count
the ways.

Box 1	Box 2
3	0
0	3
2	1
1	2

4

There are ________ different ways.

Look Back and Check

Did you find all the ways?
How did the table help you?

49

Problem-Solving Strategy: Make a Table (continued)

I. Latisha wants to give 3 bottles of juice to her friends.
    How many different choices of juice does Latisha have?
    Fill in the table to solve the problem.

Apple Juice	Grape Juice	Orange Juice
3	0	0
	3	
0	0	
2		0
	0	I
I	2	
0	2	
I	0	
		2
I		I

Latisha has ________ choices.

Name ___________________________

Problem-Solving Strategy: Make a Table

Example

Ann and Jane began reading the same book on the same day. If Ann reads 8 pages each day and Jane reads 5 pages each day, what page will Jane read on the day that Ann reads page 40?

Read and Understand

What do you know? Ann reads 8 pages per day and Jane reads 5 pages per day.

What are you trying to find? What page Jane will be reading when Ann is reading page 40.

Plan and Solve

What strategy will you use to solve the problem? Make a table. Jane will be reading page 25.

Day	1	2	3	4	5	6
Ann's Page	8	16	24	32	40	48
Jane's Page	5	10	15	20	25	30

Look Back and Check

Step 4: Is your answer reasonable? Yes, the table shows that on day 5 Ann is on page 40 and Jane is on page 25.

Complete the table. Solve each problem.

1. Rebecca must put 4 eggs in each basket. There are 8 baskets. How many eggs does she need? ___________

Number of Baskets	1	2	3	4	5	6	7	8
Number of Eggs	4	8						

Name ___________________________

Problem-Solving Strategy: Make a Table (continued)

Complete the table and solve each problem. Write the answer in a complete sentence.

2. Martin needs to water each tree with 3 gallons of water. How many gallons of water will he need for 7 trees?

Number of trees	1	2	3	4	5	6	7
Gallons of water							

____

3. Diego recorded the height of a bean plant. The first week, the plant was 2 inches high. The second, third, and fourth week, it was 4 inches, 6 inches, and 8 inches high. At this rate, when will the bean plant be 12 inches high?

Week	1	2	3	4	5	6	7
Height							

____

Test Prep   Circle the correct letter for the answer.

4. Sam waters his lawn every 6 days. Beth waters her lawn every 8 days. If they both water their lawns today, in how many days will they both be watering their lawns together again?

A 48 days   **C** 20 days

B 24 days   **D** 14 days

Name _______________________________

Problem-Solving Strategy
Make a Graph

Example

Did the pet store sell more large bags or more small bags of cat food?

Cat Food Sold					
	Mon	**Tue**	**Wed**	**Th**	**Fri**
Small	2	2	2	1	1
Large	2	2	2	2	2

Read and Understand

The chart shows how many bags of each size were sold.
You want to find out which size bag was sold more.

Plan and Solve

Small bags sold. 8 bags   Large bags sold. 10 bags

Make a graph. Color one box for every 2 bags sold.

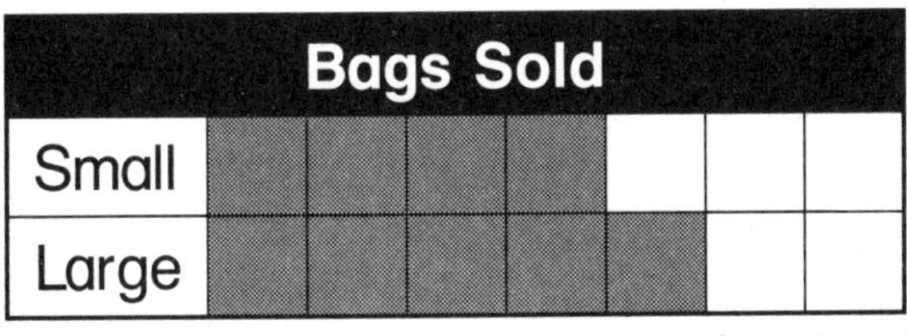

More _________ bags were sold.

1. How many more large bags were sold than
    small bags? _______________ bags

Name _______________________________

Problem-Solving Strategy: Make a Graph (continued)

Which team sold the greatest number of bags of popcorn?

Bags Sold			
Team	Week 1	Week 2	Week 3
Red	10	5	10
Blue	5	5	10
Green	10	5	5

2. You want to find which team sold the ______________ number of bags of popcorn.

Use the information in the chart to make a graph.

3. Make a graph. Color one space for every 5 bags of popcorn sold.

Bags Sold							
Red Team							
Blue Team							
Green Team							

0 5 10 15 20 25 30 35

4. Which team sold the most? ______________

5. How many bags did the team sell? ______________

Name _______________________________

Problem-Solving Strategy: Make a Graph

Example

The table lists the types of books Abby read over the summer. How many more fiction books did she read than science fiction?

Type of Book	Number
Mystery	5
Science fiction	2
Nonfiction	3
Fiction	7
History	4

Read and Understand

You know the number of books Abby read.

You need to find how many more fiction books Abby read than science fiction books.

Plan and Solve

Make a graph to solve the problem. A bar graph helps to compare data.

Abby read 5 more fiction books than science fiction books.

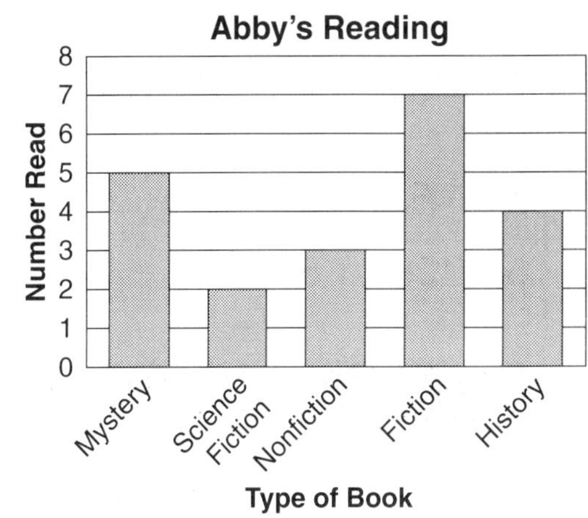

Look Back and Check

Look back and check to see if the answer is reasonable.

Solve. Write the answer in a complete sentence.

1. Use the graph above to answer the question. How many books did Abby read all summer?

____

2. How many more fiction books did Abby read then history books?

____

Name _______________________________________

Problem-Solving Strategy: Make a Graph (continued)

Solve. Write the answer in a complete sentence.

Greg took a survey of the number of third-grade runners at three schools in his town.

School	Number of Runners
Fairfield	12
Lincoln	20
Park	18

3. Draw the bars in the graph.

4. Which school has the most runners?

____

5. How many runners are there in total at all three schools?

____

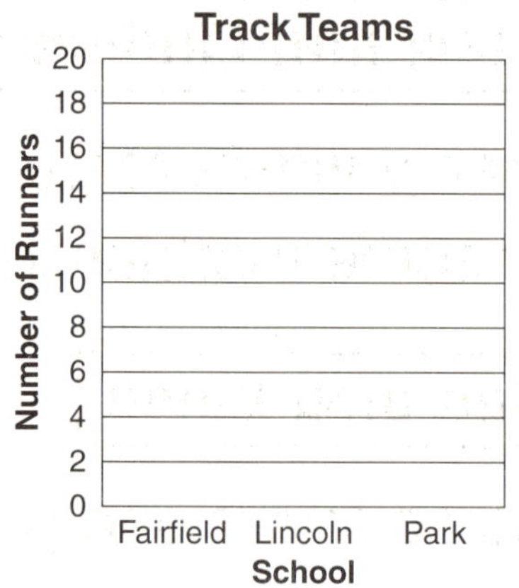

6. The table shows the number of people visiting different zoo animals. Make a bar graph of the data.

Animal	Number of Visitors
Monkeys	20
Polar Bears	32
Reptiles	15
Lions	24
Fish	12

Test Prep Circle the correct letter for the answer.

7. How many more people visited the monkeys than the fish?

A 6   **B** 8   **C** 10   **D** 12

Name ______________________________

Problem-Solving Strategy: Use Objects

Example

How can Jeremy put 9 marbles in 3 bags?

Read and Understand

Jeremy wants to put all 9 marbles in the bags. He wants to put some marbles in each bag.

Plan and Solve

Use counters and pieces of paper. Write the numbers to show one way you find.

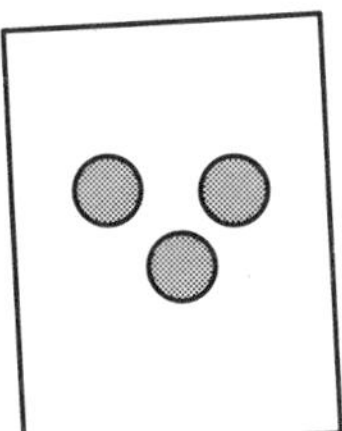 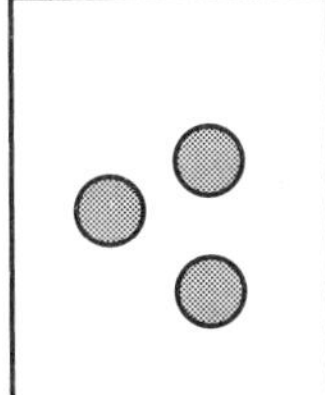 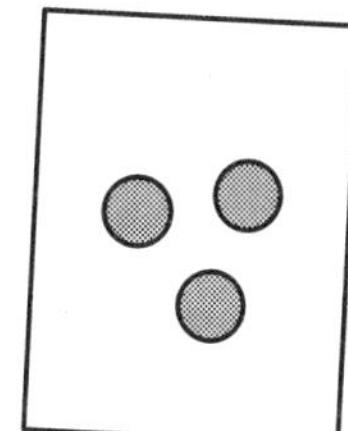

9 is ___3___ and ___3___ and ___3___ .

Look Back and Check

How do you know your answer is correct?

What is one other way to put 9 marbles in 3 bags?

1. 9 is _______ and _______ and _______ .

57

Name ___________________________________

Problem-Solving Strategy: Use Objects (continued)

How many ways can you put 10 balls into 3 boxes? Here is one
way.

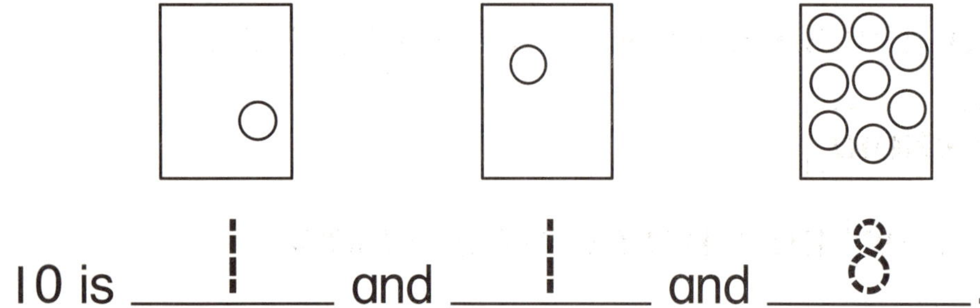

10 is ____1____ and ____1____ and ____8____.

What other ways can you find? Use counters for balls. Use
pieces of paper for boxes. Write the number sentences.

2.   10 is _________ and _________ and _________.

3.   10 is _________ and _________ and _________.

4.   10 is _________ and _________ and _________.

5.   10 is _________ and _________ and _________.

6.   10 is _________ and _________ and _________.

7.   **Reasoning** Which number is one way to write 3 and 4
     and 4? Circle the answer.

     10   11

58

Name _______________________________________

Problem-Solving Strategy: Act It Out

Example

Math starts at 2:00. It lasts one hour. When does it end?

Read and Understand

Find out what time it will be 1 hour after 2 o'clock.

Plan and Solve

 Move the minute hand around the clock one time to show 1 hour has passed. 

____**2**____ o'clock ⟶ 1 hour ⟶ ____**3**____ o'clock

Look Back and Check

Check your work. Does your answer make sense?

Write the ending time. Draw the hands on the clock.

1.

____**5**____ o'clock ⟶ 1 hour ⟶ ____ o'clock

Problem-Solving Strategy: Act It Out (continued)

Use a clock. Write the starting time and the ending time.
Then draw the hands on the clock to show the ending time.

2.

____ o'clock ⟶ I hour ⟶ ____ o'clock

3.

____ o'clock ⟶ I hour ⟶ ____ o'clock

4.

____ o'clock ⟶ 3 hours ⟶ ____ o'clock

5. **Writing in Math** Write about something you do that
takes I hour. ______________________________

____

Name _______________________________

Problem-Solving Strategy: Act It Out

Example

Wanda carries a stack of 17 books. Lyle carries a stack of
11 books. How many books should Wanda give Lyle so they
carry the same number?

Read and Understand

What do you know? Wanda has 17 books. Lyle has
11 books.

What are you trying to find? Find the number of books that
Wanda should give Lyle, so they have the same number.

Plan and Solve

What strategy will you use to solve the problem? Act it out by
placing 17 books in one pile and 11 books in another pile.
Move one book at a time from Wanda's pile to Lyle's pile until
they are equal.

When Wanda gives one to Lyle, she will have 16 and Lyle will
have 12. When she gives him a second book, she will have 15
and Lyle will have 13. When she gives him a third book, they
will both have 14 books. Wanda should give Lyle 3 books.

Look Back and Check

Is your answer reasonable? Yes, the piles of books are now equal.

Solve each problem. Write the answer in a complete sentence.

1. Bill, Phillip and Mandy each have 7 baseball cards.
   Suppose Bill gives 3 of his to Phillip, and Phillip gives
   2 of his to Mandy. How many cards does Phillip have? _______________

Name _______________________________________

Problem-Solving Strategy: Act It Out (continued)

Solve each problem.

2. David wants to make a flower garden by enclosing it with landscape timbers. If a landscape timber is 8 ft long, and he has 6 timbers, what is the maximum area of garden space he can enclose?

____

3. A sporting goods store would like to display a new line of tennis balls in a triangular stack. The bottom row will have 7 canisters and each row going up will have one less canister. How many canisters will be on display?   ___________

4. The Harris children collect snow globes. Jill has 5, Brad has 7, and Tracey has 6, but 3 of hers broke when the family moved. If Mrs. Harris asks the children to share the snow globes equally, how many will each child get?   ___________

5. The Oak Street Theater has 4 sections of seating. Each section has 5 rows of seats. Two sections have 4 seats in each row. The other sections have 3 seats in each row. How many seats are there in the theater?   ___________

6. Jeremy and Frank both collect trading cards. Jeremy has enough allowance to buy 6 each week and Frank's parents allow him to buy 4 each week. How many trading cards will Jeremy have when Frank has 36?   ___________

Test Prep Circle the correct letter for the answer.

7. Andrew folds a sheet of paper in half 5 times. When he opens it up, how many sections will there be?

    A 40   **B** 32   **C** 16   **D** 8

Name _______________________________

Problem-Solving Strategy
Look for a Pattern

Example

Read and Understand

There are 5 bicycles in the yard.
Each bicycle has 2 wheels.
How many wheels are there in the yard altogether?

Plan and Solve

You need to find out how many total wheels there are.

Make a table to
show a pattern.

Number of Bicycles	1	2	3	4	5
Number of Wheels	2	4	6	8	10

There are 10 wheels in the yard altogether.

Look Back and Check

Check your work. Does your answer make sense?

Find the pattern.
Write the numbers.

Number of Boxes	1	2		
Number of Pencils	5			

1. There are 4 boxes. Each box has 5 pencils.
    How many pencils are there in all?

    There are _______ pencils in all.

Name ________________________________

Problem-Solving Strategy: Look for a Pattern (continued)

Find the pattern. Write the numbers.

2. There are 5 sheep.
Each sheep gives
3 bags of wool.
How many bags of wool in all?

Number of Sheep	1	2			
Number of Bags	3	6			

There are _______ bags of wool in all.

3. There are 4 cats.
Each cat has 4 paws.
How many paws in all?

Number of Cats	1			
Number of Paws	4			

The cats have _______ paws in all.

4. **Reasoning** If there are 5 cats, how
many paws do they have altogether? _______________

64

Name _______________________________________

Problem-Solving Strategy: Look for a Pattern

Example

What will the next picture of dots look like?

Read and Understand

What do you know? The number of dots in each picture or row.
What are you trying to find? How the next picture of dots will
look.

Plan and Solve

What strategy will you use? Look for a pattern.
There are 2 more dots in the second picture than in the first picture.
There are 3 more dots in the third picture than in the second picture.
The number of dots added to the picture, increases by 1 each time.

There will be 4 dots in the next picture.

Look Back and Check

Is your answer reasonable? Yes, the number of dots added
increases by 1 each time.

Complete the pattern.

1. 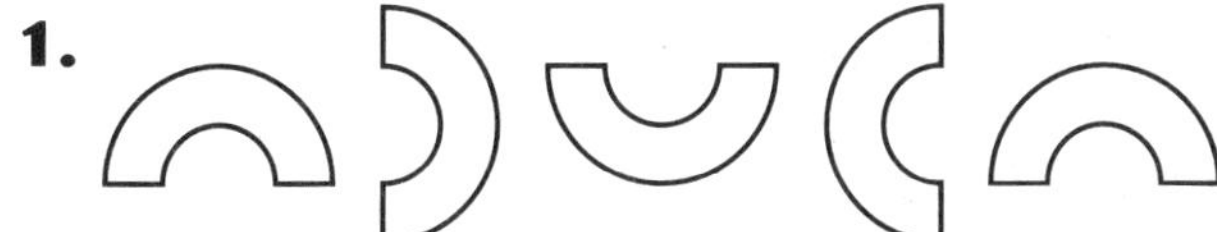

Problem-Solving Strategy: Look for a Pattern (continued)

2. What letter comes next in the
pattern?

DEEDEEDEEDE

____

3. What are the next two numbers
in the pattern 7, 10, 17, 20, 27,
30?

____

4. Paul lives at 413 Market Street. Pete lives next door at
411 Market Street, and Ted lives next door to Pete at
409 Market Street. Matt lives two doors down from Pete.
What is Matt's address?

____

5. Describe the pattern.

____

6. Amanda received 3 new customers on her paper route in
January. In February, she received 6 new customers. In
March, she received 9 new customers. If this pattern
continues, how many customers should she expect to
receive in May?

____

Test Prep Circle the correct letter for the answer.

7. What are the next two numbers in the pattern?
12, 17, 22, 27, 32, 37, …

   A 38, 39   **B** 40, 45   **C** 47, 57   **D** 42, 47

8. What are the next two numbers in the pattern
50, 48, 46, 44, 42, 40?

   A 52, 53   **B** 38, 36   **C** 39, 37   **D** 40, 36

Name _______________________

Problem-Solving Strategy
Try, Check, and Revise

Example

Maddie bought 2 items at the school store.
Together they cost 10¢.
Which items did she buy?

Read and Understand

Pick two items. Find their total.

Plan and Solve

Try:  and ERASER .

Test: 7¢ + 4¢ = 11¢

Find an item that costs less than  .

The  costs less. Try: and ERASER .

Test: $\underline{\quad 6 \quad}$ ¢ + $\underline{\quad 4 \quad}$ ¢ = $\underline{\quad 10 \quad}$ ¢

Maddie bought the 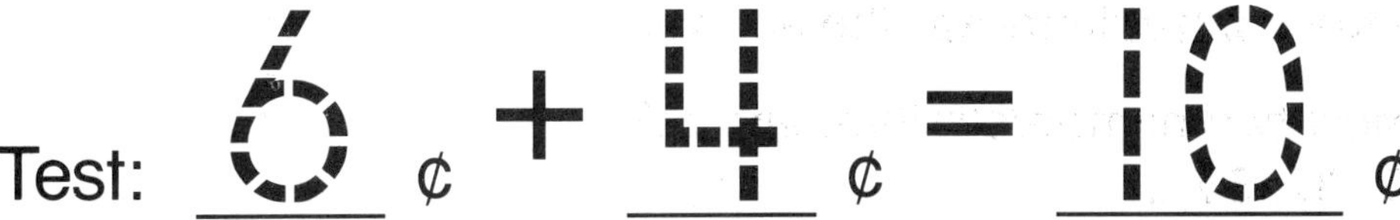 and ERASER .

Look Back and Check

How can you check your answer?

Name ______________________________

Problem-Solving Strategy: Try, Check, and Revise (continued)

Circle the toys each child bought.

Then write the number sentence to check your guess.

 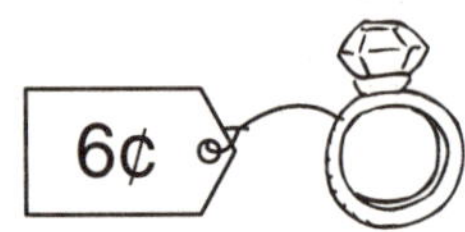 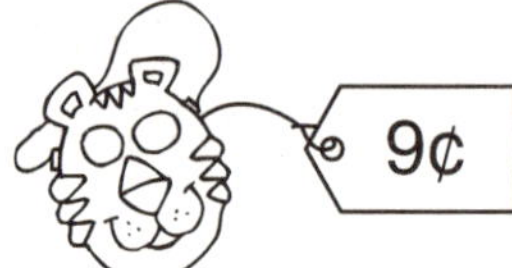 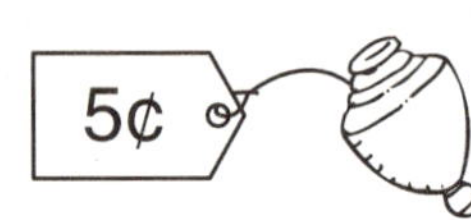

---

1. Javier bought 2 different toys.

    Together they cost 11¢.

    _____ + _____ = _____ ¢

    What did he buy? ______________________________

---

2. May-Li bought 2 different toys.

    Together they cost 16¢.

    _____ + _____ = _____ ¢

    What did she buy? ______________________________

---

3. **Writing in Math** You have one dime and one nickel. You
    want to spend the entire amount. How can you find which
    2 toys you can buy?

    ____

    ____

    ____

68

Problem-Solving Strategy
Try, Test, and Revise

Example

Ellie bought 1 bracelet and 1 charm. The bracelet cost twice as
much as the charm. If Ellie spent $0.36, what was the cost of
the charm?

Read and Understand

What do you know? Ellie spent $0.36 on 1 bracelet and
1 charm. The bracelet was twice as much as the charm.

What are you trying to find? Find the cost of 1 charm.

Plan and Solve

What strategy will you use? Try, check, and revise

1st Try	2nd Try	3rd Try
Charm: $0.10 Bracelet: $0.20 Total: $0.30	Charm: $0.11 Bracelet: $0.22 Total: $0.33	Charm: $0.12 Bracelet: $0.24 Total: $0.36
Not enough. Revise the price up 1¢.	Not enough. Revise the price up 1¢.	Correct!

Ellie bought the charm for $0.12 and the bracelet for $0.24.

Look Back and Check

Is your answer reasonable? Yes, the sum is $0.36.

Try, check, and revise to solve the problem.

1. Don has 10 sports cards in all. He has 2 more baseball
cards than football cards. How many of each card does he
have?

Name ______________________________

Problem-Solving Strategy: Try, Test, and Revise (continued)

Use the data in the table for Questions 2–4.

Camping Town	
Sleeping bag	$10
Flashlight	$3
Lantern	$5
Canteen	$4
Dried food	$2

2. Karen bought 2 different items. She spent $8. Which items did she buy?

____

3. Jake bought 3 different items. He spent a total of $15. Which items did he buy?

____

4. Adam spent $19 at Camping Town on 4 items. Two of his items were the same. What did he buy?

____

5. Gina has twice as many goldfish as zebra fish. Together, there are 42 of these fish in her tank. How many goldfish and zebra fish does she have?

____

6. Josh delivers pizza. In his money pouch are 6 bills worth $18. If he only has $1 and $5 bills, how many of each bill does he have?

____

Test Prep Circle the correct letter for the answer.

7. Mr. Gray's class has 24 students. He has three times as many girls as boys in the class. How many girls are in the class?

A 6　　　　**B** 10　　　　**C** 16　　　　**D** 18

Name ______________________________

Problem-Solving Strategy
Write a Number Sentence

Example

Read and Understand

There are 14 children on the swim team. 5 of the children are boys. How many girls are on the team?

Plan and Solve

You need to find out how many girls are on the team.

You know there are 14 children on the team and that 5 of the children are boys.

Subtract the number of boys to find the number of girls.

Write a number sentence to solve.

14 — 5 = 9 girls

Look Back and Check

Check your work. Does your answer make sense?

Write a number sentence to solve the problem.

1. Jess has 8 baseball cards.
    He has 4 basketball cards.
    How many cards does he have in all?

    ____ (+) ____ (=) ____   ____ cards

**Problem-Solving Strategy
Write a Number Sentence** (continued)

Write a number sentence to solve each problem.

2. Marcia made 7 bracelets.

    She gave 3 bracelets to her friends.

    How many bracelets does she have left?

    ___ ◯ ___ ◯ ___   ___ bracelets

3. The red team won 15 games.

    The white team won 8 games.

    How many more games did the red team win?

    ___ ◯ ___ ◯ ___   ___ games

Use the table to help you solve Questions 4–5.

Players	Game 1	Game 2
Harvey	5	7
Juanita	8	4

4. How many points did Harvey score altogether
    in Games 1 and 2?

    ___ ◯ ___ ◯ ___ points

5. How many more points did Juanita score in
    Game 1 than Harvey?

    ___ ◯ ___ ◯ ___ points

Name ______________________________

Problem-Solving Strategy
Write a Number Sentence

Example

For a school bake sale, you would like to make brownies and cupcakes. How many eggs do you need to make both treats?

Bake Goods	Number of Eggs
Brownies	3
Cookies	2
Cupcakes	2

Read and Understand

What do you know? You need 3 eggs to make brownies and 2 eggs to make cupcakes.

What are you trying to find? The total number of eggs you need to make both recipes.

Plan and Solve

What strategy will you use to solve the problem? Write a number sentence. Let e stand for the total number of eggs you need to make both treats. Solve for e.

$e = 3 + 2$

You will need 5 eggs for both recipes.

Look Back and Check

Is your answer reasonable? Yes, 3 eggs + 2 eggs = 5 eggs.

Solve each problem. Write your answer in a complete sentence.

1. Mr. and Mrs. Gordon have 11 grandsons and 5 granddaughters. How many grandchildren do the Gordons have?

____

Problem-Solving Strategy
Write a Number Sentence (continued)

2. Maggie wants to buy a set of paints for her art class. The cost of the paints is $49. She has saved $17 from her allowance so far. How much more money does she need to buy the set of paints?

____

3. Mr. Kerr wants to buy circus tickets for his family. Tickets cost $7 each. How much will it cost to buy 6 tickets?

____

4. Amy and Todd have blown up 34 balloons for a birthday party. Amy has blown up 18 balloons. How many did Todd blow up?

____

5. The McKay family needs to drive 212 miles to reach the beach for a family vacation. If they have traveled 85 miles, how many more miles do they need to travel?

____

6. There are 56 students signed up for a dance class at Jarvis Dance studio. The students are divided into groups of 8. How many groups are in the dance class?

____

Test Prep Circle the correct letter for the answer.

7. The Bulldogs basketball team scored 38 points in the first half of the game. In the second half of the game the team scored 46 points. How many points did the Bulldogs score in the entire game?

A 12   **B** 61   **C** 74   **D** 84

Problem-Solving Strategy
Use Logical Reasoning

Example

Predict: Will you need more  or more 
to measure the pencil?

Read and Understand

You need to find out if you need more  or more  .

Plan and Solve

Use reasoning to help you predict. The paper clip is shorter,
so you will need more paper clips.

Predict: (more paper clip)   more 

Look Back and Check

Measure to check.   about 5 paper clip   about 4 eraser

---

1. Will it take **fewer** paper clip or **fewer** eraser ?
    Circle your prediction. Then measure.

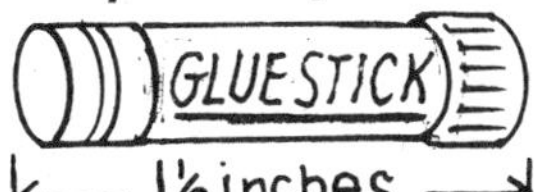

Measure to check. about ____ 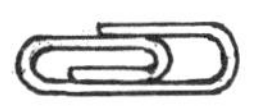 about ____ 

Problem-Solving Strategy: Use Logical Reasoning (continued)

Circle your prediction. Then measure.

2. Will it take **more**  or **more** ⬛ to measure?

Measure

about _____ 🖇

about _____ ⬛

3. Will it take **fewer** 🖇 or **fewer** ⬛ to measure?

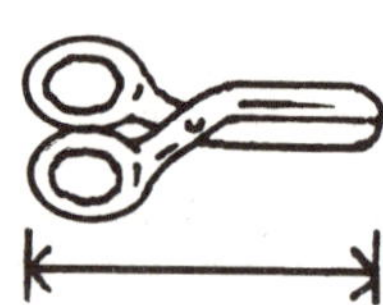

Measure

about _____ 🖇

about _____ ⬛

4. **Reasoning** Does your desk measure fewer
than or more than 15 paper clips long? ________

Name ___________________________________

Problem-Solving Strategy
Use Logical Reasoning

Example

Helen, Paula, and Tammy go to a baseball game. They bought popcorn, a hotdog, and a taco for a snack. None of the girls ate food that begins with the same letter as her name. Paula did not eat a taco. Who ate which snack?

Read and Understand

What do you know? Three girls attended a baseball game and each had a snack.

What are you trying to find? Find the snack each girl ate.

Plan and Solve

What strategy will you use to solve the problem? Use logical reasoning. Make a chart with the information you are given. Helen had the taco, Paula had the hotdog, and Tammy had the popcorn.

	Helen	Paula	Tammy
Popcorn	No	No	**Yes**
Hotdog	No	**Yes**	No
Taco	**Yes**	No	No

Look Back and Check

Is your answer reasonable? Yes, the information led to the right conclusions.

Use logical reasoning to solve the problem.

1. Nancy is thinking of a number. It is between 52 and 64. It does not have a 5 in the tens place. The sum of its digits is 9. _______

Problem-Solving Strategy: Use Logical Reasoning (continued)

Use logical reasoning to solve each problem.

2. Abby, Bill, Cara, and Dick have dentist appointments today. Each appointment is 30 minutes long. Abby's appointment is at 10:30. Bill's appointment is the last one before lunch. Cara's appointment is 1 hour after Dick's. What time is Dick's appointment? What time is Cara's?

____

3. Gary, Neil and Kyle just finished their lunch. One of the boys had a ham sandwich, another had a turkey sandwich, and the third, a chicken sandwich. Use the clues to find who ate what for lunch?

	Gary	Neil	Kyle
Ham			
Turkey		yes	
Chicken			

Kyle is allergic to ham.

Neil did not have the chicken.

Gary always eats ham.

____

4. The spring concert will be in May. Complete the calendar to find the date of the spring concert.

The concert will be on a weekend.

The date of the concert has 2 digits.

The sum of the digits is 3.

May						
S	M	T	W	TH	F	S
1	2	3	4	5	6	7
8	9	10	11	12	13	14
15	16	17	18	19	20	21
22	23	24	25	26	27	28
29	30	31				

____

Test Prep Circle the correct letter for the answer.

5. Joey is thinking of a number between 25 and 35. A 3 is not in the tens place. Joey's number is not even, and it is not 27.

A 25 **B** 26 **C** 28 **D** 29

78

Name ___________________________________

Problem-Solving Skill: Solve a Simpler Problem

Example

Mr. Lange cut a 25-foot rope into 12 equal-sized pieces. How many cuts did he make?

Read and Understand

What do you know? Mr. Lange has a 25-foot rope that he cut into 12 equal pieces.
What are you trying to find? How many cuts did he make?

Plan and Solve

What strategy will you use to solve the problem?
Solve simpler problems to find an answer.

How many cuts divide a 4-foot rope into 2 equal pieces? 1 cut
How many cuts divide a 6-foot rope into 3 equal pieces? 2 cuts
How many cuts divide a 10-foot rope into 5 equal pieces? 4 cuts

There is 1 less cut then the number of equal pieces needed.

It will take Mr. Lange 11 cuts to make 12 equal-size pieces.

Look Back and Check

Is your answer reasonable? Yes, 11 cuts is less than the number of equal pieces.

Solve each problem. Write the answer in a complete sentence.

1. Suppose Mr. Lange had a rope 50 feet long and wanted to cut it into 25 equal pieces. How many cuts would it take?

Problem-Solving Skill: Solve a Simpler Problem (continued)

Use the soccer information for Questions 2–5.

The Washington Stars signed up for a single elimination soccer tournament. This means that 2 teams play and the loser is eliminated. There are 8 entries in the tournament.

2. How many games would be played if 2 teams entered? ______________

3. How many games would be played if 3 teams entered? ______________

4. How many games would be played if 4 teams entered? ______________

5. How many games must be played to determine the champion? ______________

6. Six people at a party all shake hands with each other. How many handshakes is that?

____

7. During the grand opening of a craft store, every fourth customer was given a discount coupon. Every tenth customer was given a discount coupon and a gift. During the grand opening, 120 people visited the store. How many coupons and gifts were given away?

____

Test Prep Circle the correct letter for the answer.

8. Mr. Cintron needs to cut a 20-foot length of rope in half. Each length will then be cut into 5 equal lengths. How many equal lengths of rope will there be in total?

A 4   **B** 5   **C** 10   **D** 20

Name _______________________________

Problem-Solving Strategy: Work Backward

Example

Jean cuts 30 inches off a board to make a shelf. Then she cuts the rest of the board into 4 equal pieces. Each piece is 6 inches long. How long was the original board?

Read and Understand

What do you know? A board was cut into pieces; 1 piece is 30 inches long, and 4 pieces are each 6 inches long.

What are you trying to find? The length of the board before it was cut.

Plan and Solve

What strategy will you use to solve the problem? Work backward to find the answer. Add the lengths of all the pieces to find the length of the board before it was cut. Start with the last piece of information you know.

$$\underbrace{6 + 6 + 6 + 6}_{4 \text{ pieces}} + \underbrace{30}_{1 \text{ piece}} = 54$$

The original board was 54 inches long.

Look Back and Check

Is your answer reasonable? Yes, I worked backward using the lengths of the pieces.

Solve each problem.

1. Jeb bought a CD for $14.99 plus $1.19 for tax. He had $3.82 left. How much money did he have before he bought the CD?

____

Problem-Solving Strategy: Work Backward (continued)

Solve each problem.

2. Lola took 45 minutes to get ready for school. She walked to school in 20 minutes and then waited 5 minutes before the bell rang at 8:55 A.M. What time did she get out of bed that morning?

____

3. Josh picked a number. Next, he added 14, subtracted 6, and added 3. He ended with 34. What number did he pick?

____

4. There were 7 people in a bus. At the next stop, 4 women got in and 4 men got out. Of the 7 people in the bus, $\frac{4}{7}$ were women. How many women were in the bus to start?

____

5. The trip from your home to the museum takes 45 minutes. You need 1 hour and 30 minutes to tour a special exhibit in the museum. You want to finish the tour before 3:00 P.M. What is the latest time you should leave home to go to the museum?

____

Test Prep Circle the correct letter for the answer.

6. You currently have $15 in your savings account. When you started saving a few months ago, you decided to save $3 each month. It is now August 1. What month did you start saving?

    A February   **B** March   **C** April   **D** May

Name _______________________________________

Problem-Solving Skill
Use Data from a Chart

Fill in the ○ for the correct answer.

Use the chart to answers Questions 1–3.

Art Supplies		
Brushes	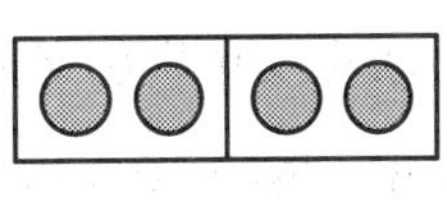	12
Pencils	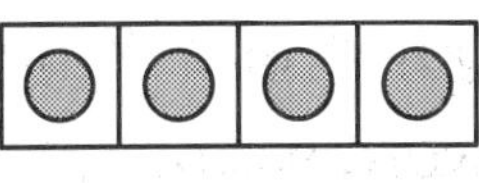	8
Paper		12
Crayons		9

1. 4 children want to share all the pencils equally.
Which shows equal shares?

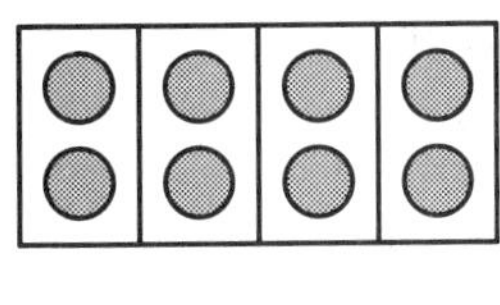   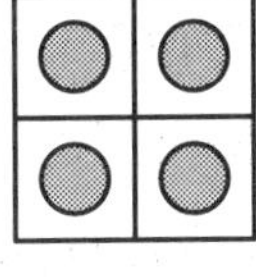

○   ○   ○   ○

2. 3 children want to share all the crayons equally. Which shows equal
shares?

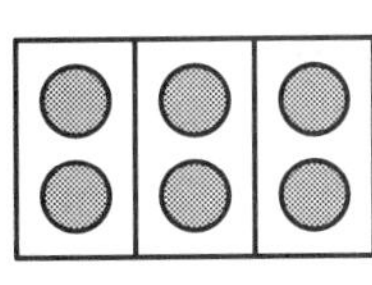   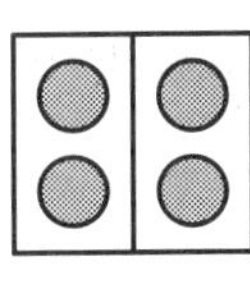   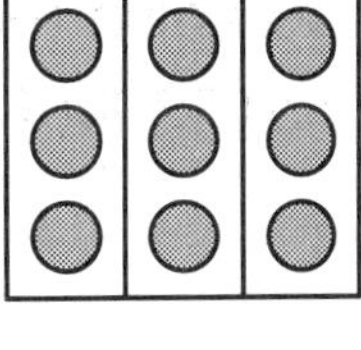   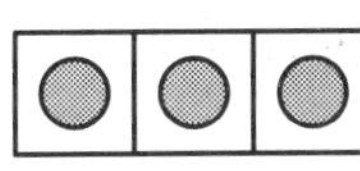

○   ○   ○   ○

3. 2 children want to share all the brushes equally. Which shows equal
shares?

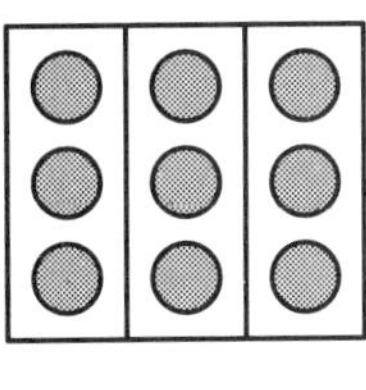   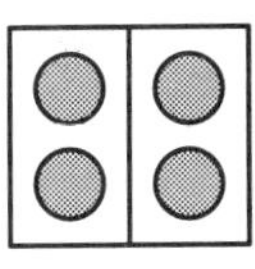   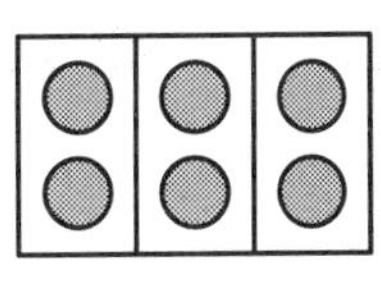   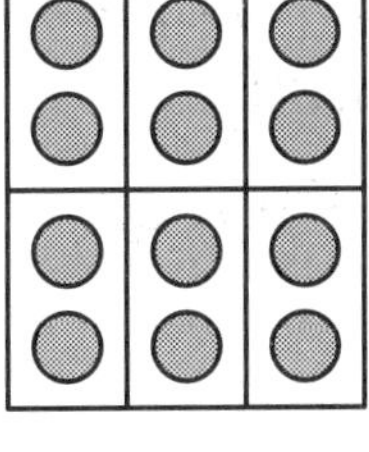

○   ○   ○   ○

Name _______________________

Problem-Solving Skill
Use Data from a Graph

Fill in the ○ for the correct answer.

Use the graph to answer Questions 1–4.

Our Toys	
Planes	
Cars	
Tops	
Trains	

1. How many planes are there?

○ 9 planes

○ 8 planes

○ 6 planes

○ 4 planes

2. Of which toy are there the fewest?

○ cars

○ planes

○ tops

○ trains

3. Of which toy are there the most?

○ trains

○ planes

○ cars

○ tops

4. How many more cars are there than planes?

○ 1 car

○ 2 cars

○ 4 cars

○ 6 cars

84

Name ___________________________________

Problem-Solving Skill
Using Data from a Picture

Fill in the ○ for the correct answer.

---

1. If the pattern continues down for 1 more row of 5 tiles, how many gray tiles will there be?

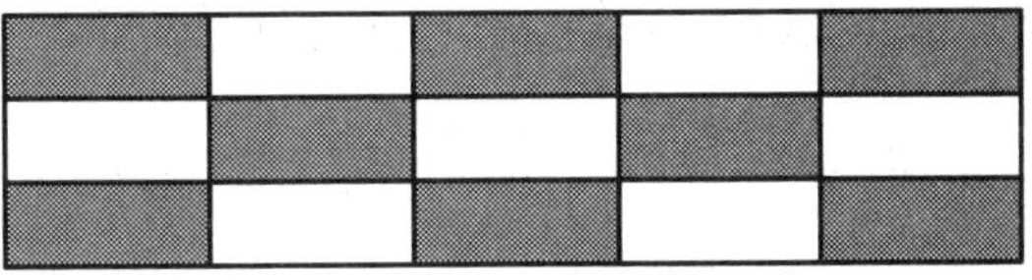

8 gray tiles
○

9 gray tiles
○

10 gray tiles
○

13 gray tiles
○

---

2. If the pattern of gray and white triangles continues for 6 more triangles, how many white triangles will there be in all?

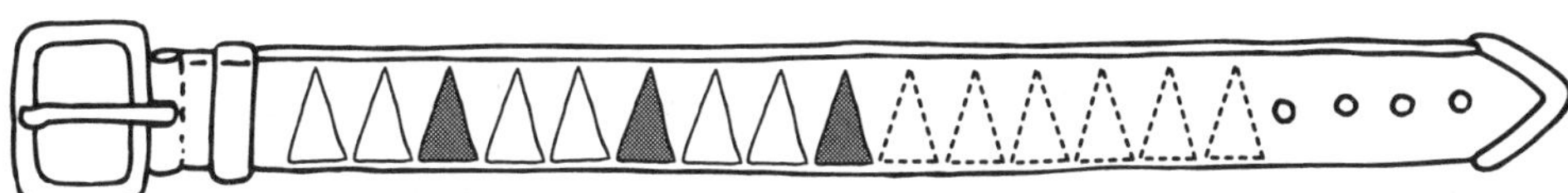

○　12 white triangles

○　10 white triangles

○　8 white triangles

○　4 white triangles

---

3. If the pattern of white and gray boards continues for 4 more boards, how many gray boards will there be in the fence?

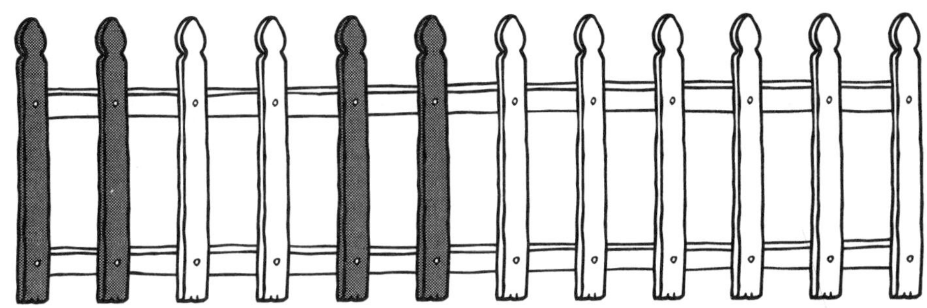

7 gray boards
○

6 gray boards
○

5 gray boards
○

4 gray boards
○

85

Problem-Solving Skill
Choose an Operation

Fill in the ○ for the correct answer.

Which number sentence solves the problem?

1. Bobby has 6 dimes. He spends 4 dimes. How many dimes does he have left?

   ○ $6 - 4 = 2$
   ○ $6 + 4 = 10$
   ○ $4 - 2 = 2$
   ○ $5 - 4 = 1$

2. Kareem has 5 coins. He gets 4 more coins. How many coins does he have in all?

   ○ $6 + 3 = 9$
   ○ $5 + 4 = 9$
   ○ $5 + 3 = 8$
   ○ $5 - 4 = 1$

3. Lisa has 7 balloons. Her friend gives Lisa 3 more balloons. How many balloons does Lisa have in all?

   ○ $7 - 3 = 4$
   ○ $7 + 3 = 10$
   ○ $7 + 2 = 9$
   ○ $6 + 3 = 9$

4. 8 kittens are in a box. 3 kittens jump out. How many kittens are left in the box?

   ○ $5 + 3 = 8$
   ○ $8 + 2 = 10$
   ○ $8 + 3 = 11$
   ○ $8 - 3 = 5$

Math Diagnosis and Intervention System

Name ______________________________

Problem-Solving Skill: Choose an Operation

Circle the correct letter for the answer.

1. Ellie has 8 shells. Alonzo has 3 times as many shells as Ellie. How many shells does Alonzo have?

   A 83
   B 24
   C 11
   D 5

2. Jimmy earns \$3 for an hour of babysitting. He earns \$5 for painting the fence. How much will Jimmy make if he baby-sits for 5 hours?

   A \$8
   B \$10
   C \$15
   D \$25

3. Ms. Jackson drove 105 miles on Wednesday and 67 miles on Thursday. Which operation must you use to find how many more miles Ms. Jackson drove on Wednesday than on Thursday?

   A addition
   B subtraction
   C multiplication
   D division

Use the data in the table for Questions 4–5.

Votes for Class President	
Student	Number of Votes
Karen	5
Jake	10
Jorge	13
Mia	6
Paul	7

4. How many more votes did Jorge get than Karen?

   A 13 votes
   B 8 votes
   C 5 votes
   D 4 votes

5. Betty received 4 times as many votes as Mia. How many votes did Betty receive?

   A 24 votes
   B 28 votes
   C 40 votes
   D 400 votes

Name ______________________________

Problem-Solving Skill
Multiple-Step Problems

Fill in the ○ for the correct answer.

Solve each problem.

1. Timo has 3 kittens. He gets 4 more. Then he sells 2 kittens. How many does he have left?

3 kittens	4 kittens	5 kittens	6 kittens
○	○	○	○

2. Sara has 10 crackers. She gives 3 to a friend. Then she gives 3 more to another friend. How many crackers does Sara have left?

3 crackers	4 crackers	5 crackers	6 crackers
○	○	○	○

3. John has 8 marbles. He loses 2 marbles. His dad gives him 4 more. How many marbles does John have now?

7 marbles	8 marbles	9 marbles	10 marbles
○	○	○	○

4. Karina has 10 carrots in her lunch. She gives 2 to one friend and 2 to another friend. How many carrots does Karina have left?

6 carrots	7 carrots	8 carrots	9 carrots
○	○	○	○

Name ______________________________

Problem-Solving Skill: Multiple-Step Problems

Circle the correct letter for the answer.

1. George bought 2 T-shirts, and Ellen bought 3 T-shirts. The T-shirts cost $7 each. What hidden question can you use to find how much they spent?

   A   What is the cost of 10 T-shirts?

   B   How many more T-shirts did Ellen buy than George?

   C   What color are the T-shirts?

   D   How many T-shirts did they buy altogether?

2. Sue is 8 years old. Fred is 3 years older than Sue. Jenna is 4 years older than Fred. How old is Jenna?

   A   11 years old

   B   15 years old

   C   16 years old

   D   44 years old

3. Mr. Smith bought 2 pounds of bananas and 4 pounds of apples. The fruit cost $2 for each pound. How much did Mr. Smith spend on fruit?

   A $4

   B $8

   C $12

   D $18

Use this table to answer Questions 4–5.

Prices for Bags of Pet Food		
	Dog	Cat
Small	$2	$1
Medium	$4	$2
Large	$6	$3

4. What is the total cost of 2 small bags of cat food and 1 large bag of cat food?

   A $2   C $7

   B $3   D $5

5. How much more do 2 medium bags of dog food cost than 2 medium bags of cat food?

   A $4   C $12

   B $8   D $16

6. Lena caught 8 fish, and Sven caught 2 fish. The fish weighed about 2 pounds each. What hidden question can you use to find how much the fish weighed in all?

   A   What is the weight of all the fish?

   B   How many more fish did Lena catch than Sven?

   C   What kind of fish did they catch?

   D   How many fish did they catch altogether?

89

Name _______________________

Problem-Solving Skill
Extra Information

Fill in the ○ for the correct answer.

What information is **not** needed to solve the problem?

1. Richard has 4 red toy airplanes. He has 2 dogs and 1 cat. He has 3 green toy airplanes. How many toy airplanes does he have in all?

- ○ Richard has 4 red toy airplanes.
- ○ He has 2 dogs and 1 cat.
- ○ He has 3 green toy airplanes.
- ○ Richard has 10 red toy airplanes.

2. Tina has 8 pairs of shoes. She gets 2 more pairs of shoes. Her favorite pair is red. How many pairs does she have now?

- ○ Tina has 8 pairs of shoes
- ○ How many pairs does she have now?
- ○ She gets 2 more pairs of shoes.
- ○ Her favorite pair is red.

Which number sentence solves the problem?

3. Timothy has 6 hamsters. 2 of the hamsters are brown. His friend gave him 3 more hamsters. How many hamsters does he have now?

- ○ $2 + 3 = 5$ hamsters
- ○ $6 + 3 = 9$ hamsters
- ○ $6 + 2 = 8$ hamsters
- ○ $6 - 2 = 4$ hamsters

4. There are 5 cars in the parking lot. 4 cars are red. 2 more cars come into the parking lot. How many cars are there now?

- ○ $5 + 2 = 7$ cars
- ○ $5 - 2 = 3$ cars
- ○ $4 + 2 = 6$ cars
- ○ $5 + 4 = 9$ cars

Name ___________________________

Problem-Solving Skill
Extra or Missing Information

Circle the correct letter for the answer.

1. Asim's room is 12 feet long and 10 feet wide. The family room is 14 feet wide. What information do you need to find how much longer the family room is than Asim's room?

   A the length of Asim's room

   B the length of the family room

   C the width of Asim's kitchen

   D the width of Sue's room

2. Marvin, Alvin, and Billy are brothers. Marvin is 10 years old. Alvin is 2 years younger than Marvin. Billy is 3 years older than Marvin. What extra information is not needed to find how old Billy is?

   A How much younger Alvin is than Marvin.

   B How old Marvin is.

   C How much older Billy is than Marvin.

   D All information is needed.

3. There will be 8 people at Lila's party. Each person will get 1 carton of juice. Juice costs \$2 per carton. Each carton fills 4 glasses. How many cartons of juice will Lila need?

   A 1 carton   **C** 4 cartons

   B 2 cartons   **D** 32 cartons

Use the sign for Questions 4 and 5.

4. Tyrone bought 3 CDs and 2 tapes. How much did he pay for the CDs?

   A \$15   **C** \$30

   B \$25   **D** \$40

5. Brittany bought some DVDs and some tapes. She spent \$40 in all. Her change was \$10. How many DVDs and tapes did Brittany buy?

   A 2 DVDs and 2 tapes

   B 3 DVDs and 2 tapes

   C 2 DVDs and 3 tapes

   D 2 DVDs and 4 tapes

Name ____

Problem-Solving Skill
Exact Answer or Estimate

Fill in the O for the correct answer.

Which response is the best answer to each question?

1. Jeremy wants to buy 4 stickers. They cost 6¢ each. About how much money does he need?

- O   estimate about 10¢
- O   estimate about 25¢
- O   exact amount of 25¢
- O   exact amount of 32¢

2. 1 apple costs 8¢. Bob pays 10¢. How much change does he get?

- O   estimate about 20¢
- O   estimate about 10¢
- O   exact amount of 2¢
- O   exact amount of 18¢

3. Sari has 7 stickers. She gets 10 more stickers. About how many stickers does she have?

- O   estimate about 20 stickers
- O   estimate about 10 stickers
- O   exact amount of 5 stickers
- O   exact amount of 3 stickers

4. 1 bagel costs 8¢. How much do 3 bagels cost?

- O   estimate about 11¢
- O   estimate about 16¢
- O   exact amount of 10¢
- O   exact amount of 24¢

Name ____

Problem-Solving Skill: Exact or Estimate?

Circle the correct letter for the answer.

1. **For which problem is an estimate enough?**

    A On Saturday, 368 people went to the zoo. On Sunday, 406 people went. Did at least 900 people go that weekend?

    B On Saturday, 368 people went to the zoo. On Sunday, 406 people went. How many people went that weekend?

    C On Saturday, 368 people went to the zoo. On Sunday, 406 people went. How many fewer people went to the zoo on Saturday than on Sunday?

    D On Saturday, 368 people went to the zoo. On Sunday, 406 people went. How many more people went to the zoo on Sunday than on Saturday?

2. **Carl is playing a computer game. The top score is 500 points. Carl's score so far is 199. How many more points does Carl need to reach the top score?**

    A exactly 201 more

    B exactly 301 more

    C at least 400 more

    D at least 500 more

3. **Box A weighs 183 pounds. Box B weighs 124 pounds. Which sentence is true?**

    A Box A weighs more than 100 pounds more than Box B.

    B Box B weighs at least 50 pounds less than Box A.

    C Box B weighs exactly 10 pounds more than Box A.

    D Box A weighs exactly 29 pounds less than Box B.

4. **A new computer costs $885. Ms. Richards has saved $598. How much more money does Ms. Richards need to buy the computer?**

    A at least $1,483 more

    B at least $900 more

    C exactly $300 more

    D exactly $287 more

Problem-Solving Skill: Read and Understand

Circle the correct letter for each answer.

1. Emily bought 2 CDs for $7 each. She bought 1 CD for $10. How much did Emily pay for the CDs?

   A $7
   B $14
   C $24
   D $34

2. In January, it snowed on 12 days. In February, it snowed on 19 days. On how many more days did it snow in February than it did in January?

   A 31 days
   B 30 days
   C 7 days
   D 6 days

3. Tanesha tossed a penny several times. The penny landed on heads 20 times. It landed on tails 30 times. How many times did Tanesha toss the penny?

   A 60 times
   B 50 times
   C 10 times
   D 3 times

4. The gas tank in Mr. Rivera's car holds 16 gallons of gas. There are 8 gallons of gas in the tank now. How many more gallons does Mr. Rivera need to put into the tank to fill it?

   A 2 gallons
   B 8 gallons
   C 14 gallons
   D 24 gallons

5. Mia collected 15 red marbles and 9 black marbles. She put 10 of the red marbles and 5 of the black marbles in a bag. How many marbles were in the bag?

   A 40 marbles
   B 20 marbles
   C 24 marbles
   D 15 marbles

6. There are 12 months in a year. Each month has a certain number of letters. Which month has the fewest letters?

   A September
   B July
   C June
   D May

Name ____

Problem-Solving Skill: Plan and Solve

Circle the correct letter for the answer.

1. Beth has 16 baseball cards. She wants to have 25 baseball cards. How many more cards does Beth need?

   A 41 cards

   B 31 cards

   C 10 cards

   D 9 cards

2. Ellie has been doing homework for 15 minutes. The time now is 4:20 P.M. At what time did Ellie start doing her homework?

   A 4:35 P.M.

   B 4:25 P.M.

   C 4:05 P.M.

   D 4:00 P.M.

3. Each box of pencils contains 10 pencils. Each carton contains 6 boxes of pencils. How many pencils are in 5 cartons?

   A 10 pencils

   B 60 pencils

   C 300 pencils

   D 3,000 pencils

4. Jackie is thinking of a number. When she adds 3 to her number and then subtracts 1 from the total, she gets 5. What number is Jackie thinking of?

   A 1   **C** 3

   B 2   **D** 4

5. Sue and Sam borrow some books from the library. Sam borrows twice as many books as Sue. Sue borrows 5 books. How many books does Sam borrow?

   A 5 books

   B 10 books

   C 20 books

   D 25 books

6. George's local swimming pool is 50 feet long. George swims for 150 feet. How many lengths of the pool is that?

   A 50 lengths

   B 10 lengths

   C 3 lengths

   D 2 lengths

Problem-Solving Skill
Look Back and Check

Solve each problem.
Write **more** or **less** to check your answers.

1. Ronald ran 7 miles.
Then he ran 6 miles.
How many miles did he run? _______ miles
Did Ronald run **more** or **less** than 7 miles? _______

2. George gave gifts to 4 friends.
He gave 2 gifts to each friend.
How many gifts did he give? _______ gifts
Did George give **more** or **less** than 4 gifts? _______

3. Alisha built 12 dollhouses.
She sold 4 dollhouses.
How many dollhouses does she have? _______ dollhouses
Did Alisha have **more** or **less** than 12 dollhouses? _______

4. Sally had 15 cups of fruit juice.
She sold 8 cups.
How many cups does she still have? _______ cups
Did Sally have **more** or **less** than 15 cups? _______

5. Glen walked 7 miles.
Stan walked 6 miles.
How many miles did they walk in all? _______ miles
Did they walk **more** or **less** than 7 miles? _______

Name ________________________________

Problem-Solving Skill: Look Back and Check

Circle the correct letter for the answer.

1. You get 3 stars for each book you read. How many stars would you get if you read 5 books?

   A 3 stars

   B 5 stars

   C 10 stars

   D 15 stars

2. Ed has 2 quarters and 7 nickels in his bank. Fred has 7 dimes and 5 nickels in his bank. Ned has 9 dimes and 7 pennies in his bank. Jed has 3 quarters and 5 pennies in his bank. Who has the most money in their bank?

   A Ed   **C** Fred

   B Ned   **D** Jed

3. Bob buys a pair of jeans. The total cost is $23. He pays with a $20 bill and a $5 bill. How much change should Bob receive?

   A $25   **C** $3

   B $23   **D** $2

4. Britney has 4 apple pies. She cuts each pie into 6 pieces. How many pieces of apple pie does Britney have?

   A 24 pieces

   B 18 pieces

   C 12 pieces

   D 6 pieces

5. It costs $1 to buy a can of soda. The machine can take only quarters and nickels. How many ways can you put $1 in the soda machine?

   A 1 way   **C** 4 ways

   B 2 ways   **D** 5 ways

6. George, Mary, and Juan are fourth-graders. George is taller than Juan. Mary is shorter than Juan. Which is the correct order of students from the tallest to the shortest?

   A George, Mary, Juan

   B George, Juan, Mary

   C Mary, George, Juan

   D Juan, George, Mary

Name _______________________

Problem-Solving Skill
Translating Words to Expressions

Circle the correct letter for the answer.

Which numerical expression matches the situation?

1. The number of tires on 3 cars when 1 car has 4 tires

   A $3 + 1$ **C** $3 + 4$

   B 3×4 **D** $4 - 3$

2. Mr. Ramirez had 45 pencils at the beginning of the year. The class used 44 pencils.

   A $45 + 44$ **C** $45 - 44$

   B $44 - 45$ **D** $45 \div 44$

3. The total of 3 cubes, 7 spheres, and 10 cylinders

   A $3 + 7 + 10$

   B $3 + 7 - 10$

   C $3 \times 7 \times 10$

   D $7 + 3 \times 10$

4. The cost of one ticket if all the tickets for 5 children cost $25 in all

   A $\$25 - 5$

   B $\$5 + \$25$

   C $\$25 \times 5$

   D $\$25 \div 5$

5. Harry has 30 stamps on 5 pages of his stamp album. There are the same number of stamps on each page.

   A 5×30

   B $30 - 5$

   C $30 + 5$

   D $30 \div 5$

6. 12 boys minus 3 boys

   A $12 - 3$

   B $3 + 3$

   C $12 \div 3$

   D $12 + 3$

7. Twenty children were singing. Then 5 children stopped singing.

   A $20 + 5$

   B 20×5

   C $20 - 5$

   D $5 - 20$

8. 4 times as tall as 8 feet

   A $4 - 8$

   B $8 - 4$

   C 4×8

   D $8 + 4$

Name _______________________________

Problem-Solving Skill: Writing to Explain

Circle the correct letter for the answer.

1. Suppose you spin the spinner below 100 times. Which letter would you spin about the same number of times as the letter A?

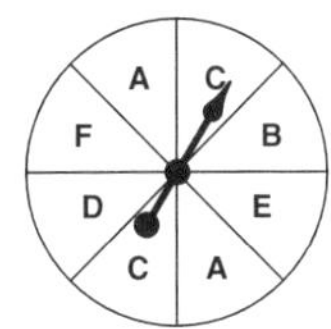

A   The letter B.

B   The letter F.

C   The letter C.

D   The letter D.

2. Su Jong has $15. Can she buy a T-shirt for $7.98 and a pair of shorts for $5.98?

A   No. The costs round to $800 and $600. $800 + $600 = $1,400, and $15 < $1,400.

B   No. The costs round to $80 and $60. $80 + $60 = $140, and $15 < $140.

C   No. The costs round to $10 and $10. $10 + $10 = $20, and $15 < $20.

D   Yes. The costs round to $8 and $6. $8 + $6 = $14, and $15 > $14.

3. Jack has 73 baseball cards and 102 basketball cards. Ron has 57 baseball cards and 296 basketball cards. Jill has 301 baseball cards and 0 basketball cards. Katie has 154 baseball cards and 51 basketball cards. Estimate who has the most cards.

A   Jack; 70 + 100 = 170

B   Ron; 60 + 300 = 360

C   Jill; 300 + 0 = 300

D   Katie; 150 + 50 = 200

4. What is the missing number?

Pennies saved	1	2	3	4	5
Nickels saved	3	6	9	12	?

A   6. The number of nickels is 1 more than the number of pennies.

B   10. The number of nickels is 2 times the number of pennies.

C   15. The number of nickels is 3 times the number of pennies.

D   20. The number of nickels is 15 more than the number of pennies.

Name ___________________________________

Problem-Solving Skill: Writing to Compare

Circle the correct letter for each answer.

---

1. Use the bar graphs below. Which comparison statement is true?

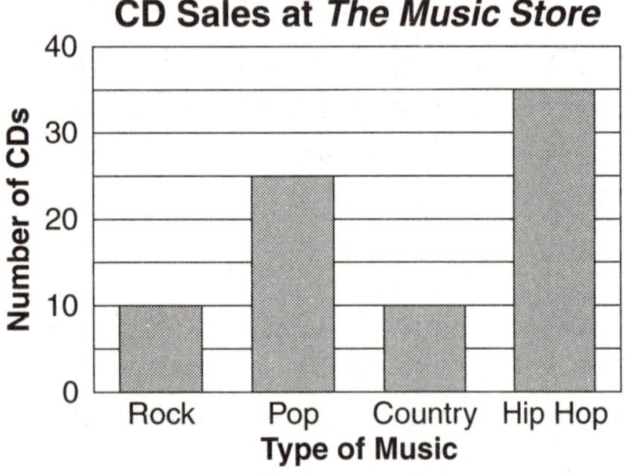

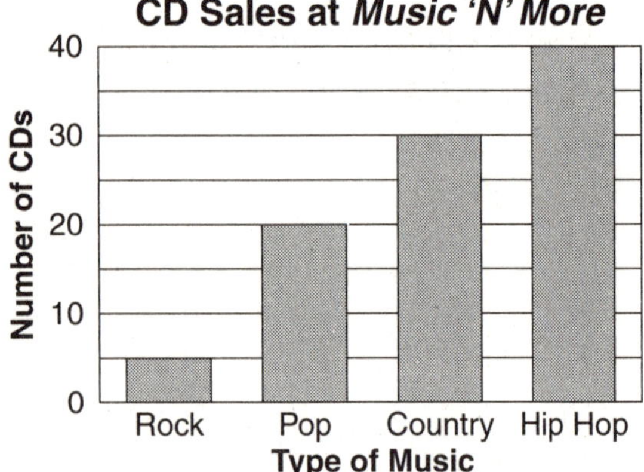

A *The Music Store* sold the same number of country CDs as *Music 'N' More* sold.

B *Music 'N' More* sold more pop CDs than *The Music Store* sold.

C *The Music Store* sold fewer rock CDs than *Music 'N' More* sold.

D Both stores sold more Hip Hop CDs than other types of CDs.

2. Betty spent $2.75 on books and $5.50 on art supplies. Jamal spent $2.90 on books and $5.25 on art supplies. Which comparison statement is true?

A Jamal spent more on art supplies than Betty did.

B Betty spent more in all than Jamal did.

C Jamal spent less on books than Betty did.

D Betty and Jamal spent the same amount in art supplies.

---

3. Jim, Ella, and Quan are reading the same book. So far Jim has read 72 pages, Ella has read 83 pages, and Quan has read 49 pages. Which comparison statement is true?

A Jim has read the most pages so far.

B Quan has read fewer pages than Ella.

C Ella and Jim have read the same number of pages.

D Quan has read more pages than Jim.

Name ______________________________

Problem Solving Strategy: Writing to Describe

Circle the correct letter for the answer.

1. Use the figures below. Which description is true?

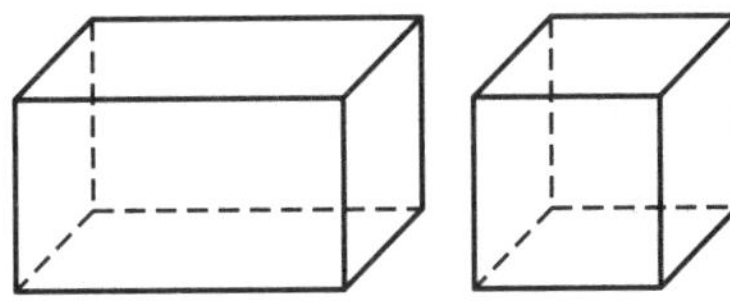

- **A** Both have twelve faces.
- **B** The rectangular prism can roll, but the cube cannot.
- **C** The cube has six square faces, but the rectangular prism does not.
- **D** Both have flat surfaces shaped like a circle.

2. Which description is true?

- **A** A quadrilateral has four sides, but a triangle has only three sides.
- **B** A rectangle and a trapezoid both have four right angles.
- **C** A rhombus has parallel sides, but a parallelogram does not.
- **D** An isosceles triangle and an equilateral triangle both have all sides the same length.

3. Which description is true?

- **A** Intersecting lines and parallel lines both cross at one point.
- **B** A right angle is greater than an acute angle but less than an obtuse angle.
- **C** A line segment and a ray both have two endpoints.
- **D** An acute angle is greater than a right angle, but an obtuse angle is less than a right angle.

4. Use the figures below. Which description is true?

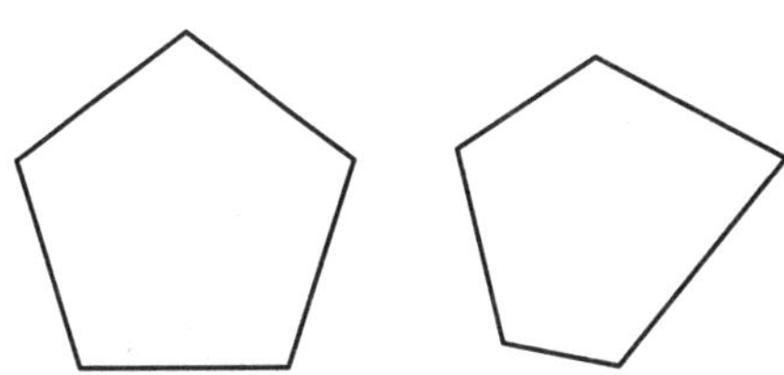

- **A** Both figures have 5 right angles.
- **B** Both figures are solid shapes.
- **C** Both figures have 4 sides.
- **D** Both figures have 5 sides.

Name ____

Problem-Solving Skills
Interpreting Remainders

Circle the correct letter for the answer.

1. Ashley has 75 stamps to put in a stamp album. Each page in the album holds 9 stamps. How many stamps will be on the page that is *not* completely filled?

   A 9 stamps

   B 8 stamps

   C 4 stamps

   D 3 stamps

2. The Johnson family is going to vacation in Florida. They are driving 6 hours each day. It takes 45 hours to drive to Florida. How many days will it take to drive to Florida?

   A 6 days   **C** 8 days

   B 7 days   **D** 10 days

3. Ellen had $30. She bought as many books as she could. If each book cost $7, how many books did Ellen buy?

   A 210 books

   B 30 books

   C 4 books

   D 2 books

Use the problem below for Questions 4 and 5.

Mia uses 4 yellow beads and 4 green beads to make a friendship bracelet. She has 25 yellow beads and 21 green beads.

4. How many bracelets can Mia make?

   A 8 bracelets

   B 7 bracelets

   C 5 bracelets

   D 3 bracelets

5. How many more green beads does Mia need to make one more bracelet?

   A 1 more

   B 2 more

   C 3 more

   D 4 more

6. Rashid is setting up tables for a school party. Each table seats 6 people. There will be 45 people at the party. How many tables will be needed?

   A 5 tables   **C** 8 tables

   B 7 tables   **D** 12 tables

Name _______________________________

Problem-Solving Strategy
Draw a Picture

Fill in the ○ for the correct answer.

Which is the picture for the problem?

1. Kareem has 4 tennis balls. Ricky has 6 tennis balls. How many tennis balls do they have in all?

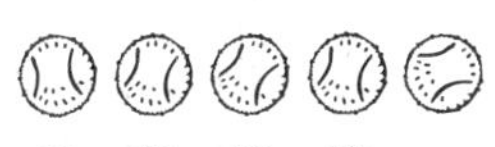
○   ○
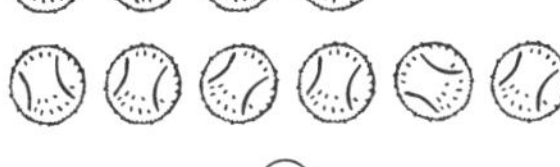

○   ○

2. Rosa has 5 stickers. Ruth has 4 stickers. How many stickers do they have in all?

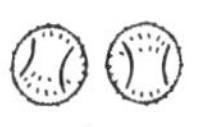

○   ○
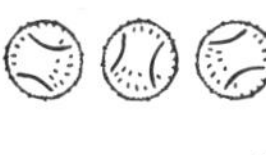

○   ○

3. Tim has 4 bird stamps. Eduardo has 3 cat stamps. How many stamps do they have in all?

○   ○

○   ○

4. Jacob has 5 stickers. Marie has 5 stickers. How many stickers do they have in all?

○   ○

○   ○

Name _______________________

Problem-Solving Strategy: Draw a Picture

Circle the correct letter for the answer.

1. If it takes 10 minutes to saw a log twice to make three pieces, how long would it take to cut the log into four pieces?

  A 3 minutes   **C** 15 minutes

  B 13 minutes   **D** 20 minutes

2. Tina is making a bracelet for her friend Sara. She puts 4 yellow beads on the chain, then 3 blue beads, then 4 yellow beads, then 3 blue beads, and so on. If she uses 16 yellow beads, then stops, how many blue beads has she used?

  A 6   **C** 12

  B 9   **D** 15

3. Four friends are waiting in line at the amusement park. Jenny is in front of Kraig. Kraig is in front of Mary. Greg is first. Who is last in line?

  A Kraig   **C** Greg

  B Mary   **D** Jenny

4. The parent's club is making breakfast for the teachers. The teachers have a choice of scrambled or fried eggs and home fries or potato wedges. They also have a choice of banana, cinnamon or pineapple bread. How many different breakfasts are there?

  A 12   **C** 6

  B 7   **D** 3

5. Mrs. Winston is installing lighting along her sidewalk. The length of her sidewalk is 18 feet and a light needs to be placed at the beginning and end of the sidewalk and every 2 feet. How many lights will Mrs. Winston need?

  A 8   **C** 10

  B 9   **D** 12

6. Carla gives herself 5 beads for each 2 beads she gives Anita. If Carla has 20 beads how many does Anita have?

  A 6   **C** 10

  B 8   **D** 12

Name ________________________________

Problem-Solving Strategy
Make an Organized List

Fill in the ○ for the correct answer.

Use the list to answer
Questions 1–3.

Ways to Make ⬢

Shapes I Used	⬡	▱	△
Way 1	1	0	0
Way 2	0	1	1
Way 3	0	0	3

1. How many ways are there to make this shape?

3 ways ○   2 ways ○   0 ways ○   4 ways ○

2. How many △ can make this shape?

0 △ ○   3 △ ○   1 △ ○   4 △ ○

3. Which way uses 2 different shapes to make this shape?

Way 1 ○   Way 2 ○   Way 3 ○   No Way ○

105

Name ___________________________________

Problem-Solving Strategy
Make an Organized List

Circle the correct letter for the answer.

1. A cafeteria serves 3 types of noodles with either meat or tomato sauce. How many different dinners of noodles with sauce can you make?

   A 3   **C** 9
   B 6   **D** 12

2. Matthew is going fishing. He will use worms and minnows for bait. He has 5 fishing poles. How many bait and fishing pole combinations can he use?

   A 1   **C** 10
   B 5   **D** 15

3. Your mom offers sundaes for dessert. You can choose vanilla or strawberry frozen yogurt with a topping of nuts, coconut, fruit, or chocolate sauce. If you can have one flavor of yogurt and one topping, how many choices do you have for a sundae?

   A 4   **C** 8
   B 6   **D** 10

4. A candle-making kit contains 5 scents and 4 colors of wax. How many combinations of candles can you create using one color and one scent?

   A 4   **C** 9
   B 5   **D** 20

5. Sofia's Café offers a brunch special of eggs and your choice of bacon, sausage links, or sausage patties. You can order your eggs scrambled, fried, or poached. How many different combinations of the brunch special are possible?

   A 9   **C** 15
   B 12   **D** 18

6. Maria needs to do her chores. She has to make her bed, water the plants, sweep the kitchen, and dust the living room. In how many different orders can she do her chores?

   A 8   **C** 24
   B 12   **D** 48

Name ______________________________

Problem-Solving Strategy Make a Table

Fill in the ○ for the correct answer.

Sean eats 3 fruits each day. He never eats 3 of the **same** fruit. The table shows different fruits Sean eats in 4 days. Finish the table.

Fruits	Banana	Apple	Orange
Day 1	■	1	0
Day 2	2	■	1
Day 3	0	2	■
Day 4	0	■	2

1. How many bananas did Sean eat on Day 1?

○ 1 banana ○ 0 bananas ○ 2 bananas ○ 3 bananas

2. How many apples did Sean eat on Day 2?

○ 2 apples ○ 4 apples ○ 0 apples ○ 3 apples

3. How many oranges did Sean eat on Day 3?

○ 5 oranges ○ 2 oranges ○ 3 oranges ○ 1 orange

4. How many apples did Sean eat on Day 4?

○ 1 apple ○ 3 apples ○ 2 apples ○ 4 apples

Name ______________________

Problem-Solving Strategy: Make a Table

Circle the correct letter for the answer.

1. Jacob and Mark each began biking today. If Jacob bikes 4 miles each day and Mark bikes 6 miles each day, how many miles will Jacob have biked when Mark has biked 30 miles?

   A   16 miles   **C**   24 miles
   B   20 miles   **D**   28 miles

2. Nicholas needs to place 6 cups on each table for the picnic. If there are 8 tables, how many cups will he need?

   A   14   **C**   52
   B   48   **D**   58

3. Lee made the same number of birdhouses each day. Which number will complete the table for the number of birdhouses Lee has completed during 4 days?

Day	1	2	3	4
Birdhouses	7	14	21	?

   A   42   **C**   36
   B   32   **D**   28

4. Lydia recorded the height of a sunflower. The first week, the plant was 3 inches high. The second, third, and fourth week, it was 5 inches, 7 inches, and 9 inches high. At this rate, when will the sunflower be 15 inches high?

   A   5 weeks   **C**   6 weeks
   B   7 weeks   **D**   8 weeks

5. Jenna bakes cookies every third day. Her best friend Wanda bakes cookies every fourth day. If they both baked cookies today, in how many days will they both be baking cookies again?

   A   7 days   **C**   9 days
   B   12 days   **D**   15 days

6. Max needs to water each of his pepper plants with 2 cups of water. How many cups of water will he need for 5 pepper plants?

   A   7 cups
   B   10 cups
   C   12 cups
   D   14 cups

Name ________________________

Problem-Solving Strategy
Make a Graph

Fill in the ○ for the correct answer.

Use the information in the graph to answer the questions.

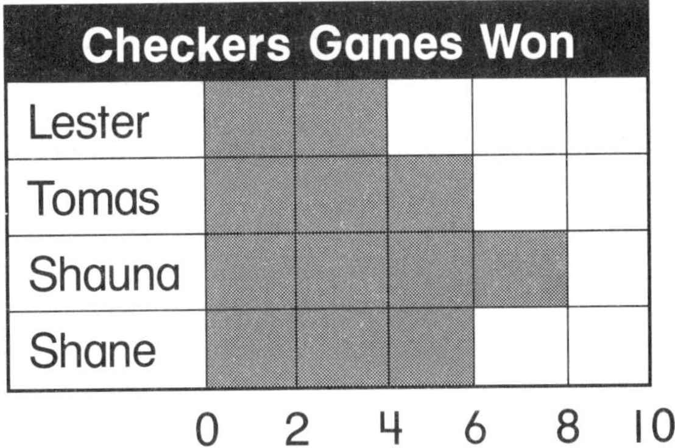

I. How many games did Lester win?

2 games   4 games   6 games   8 games
○   ○   ○   ○

2. How many games did Tomas win?

6 games   2 games   10 games   4 games
○   ○   ○   ○

3. Who won the most games?

Lester   Shauna   Tomas   Shane
○   ○   ○   ○

Name ___________________________

Problem-Solving Skill: Make a Graph

Circle the correct letter for the answer.

Use the graph for Questions 1–3.

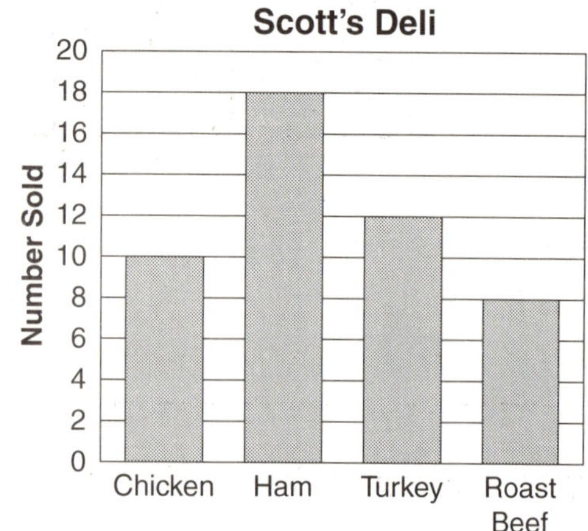

1. How many chicken sandwiches were sold?

A 8 **C** 10
B 12 **D** 18

2. How many more turkey sandwiches were sold than roast beef?

A 12 **C** 8
B 6 **D** 4

3. How many more of the most popular sandwich were sold than the least popular?

A 18 **C** 12
B 10 **D** 8

Use the graph for Questions 4–6.

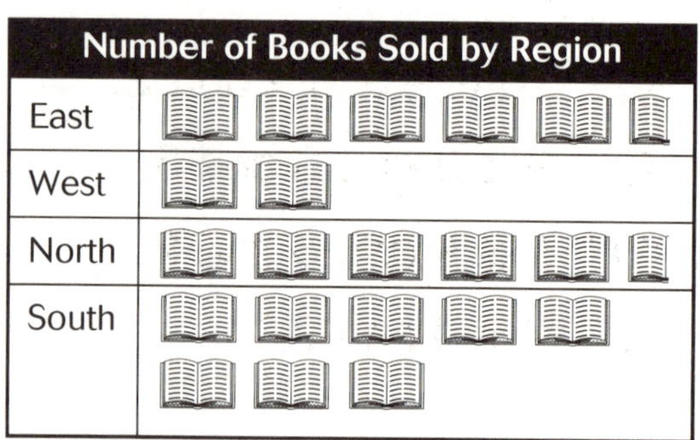

Key: Each represents 10 books each.

4. Which region sold the most books?

A East **C** West
B North **D** South

5. How many books were sold in the West?

A 2 **C** 10
B 20 **D** 30

6. How many more books were sold in the South than the North?

A 80 **C** 55
B 25 **D** 20

7. How many total books were sold?

A 220 **C** 210
B 200 **D** 21

Problem-Solving Strategy: Use Objects

Fill in the ○ for the correct answer.

1. This picture shows which number sentence?

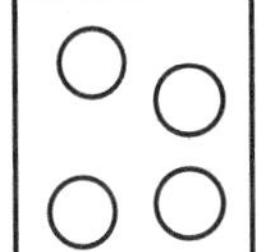 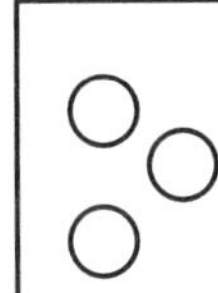 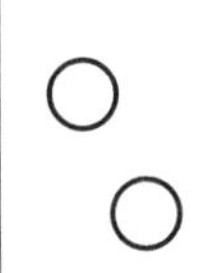

   ○   10 is 4 and 4 and 2.

   ○   9 is 3 and 3 and 3.

   ○   9 is 4 and 3 and 2.

   ○   7 is 4 and 3.

2. Which picture shows how to put 8 balls into 2 boxes?

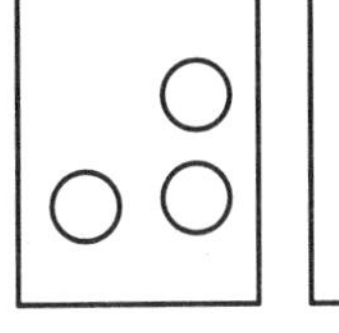 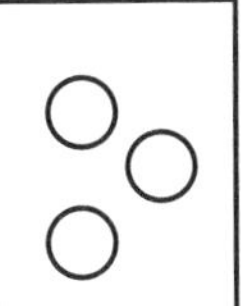   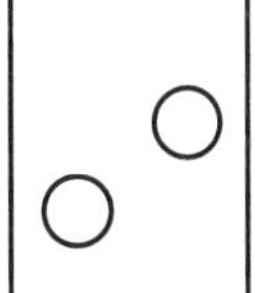 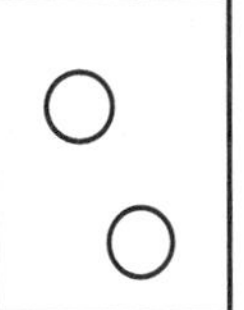 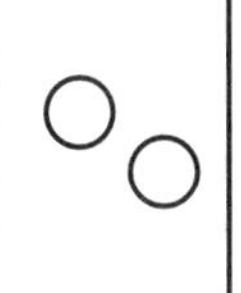 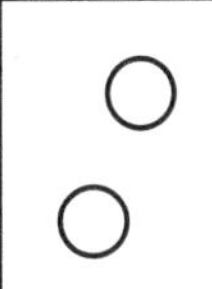

○   ○

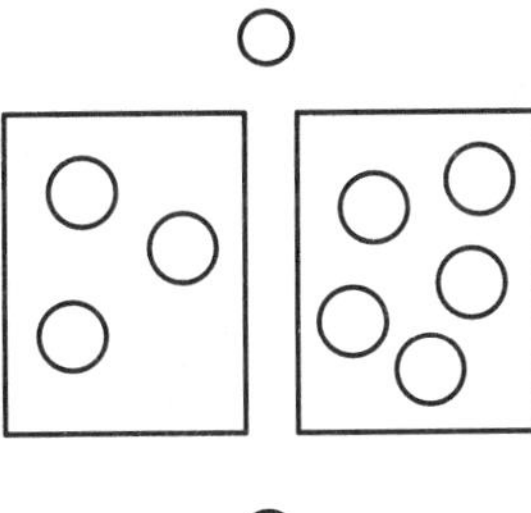    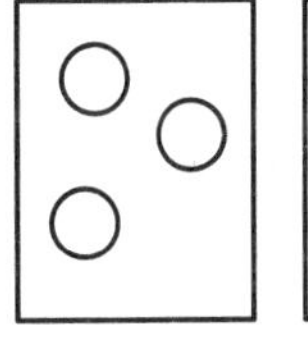 

○   ○

3. This picture shows which number sentence?

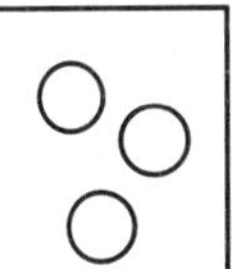 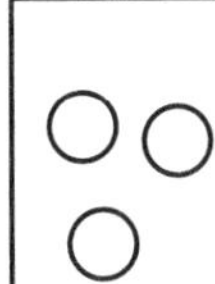 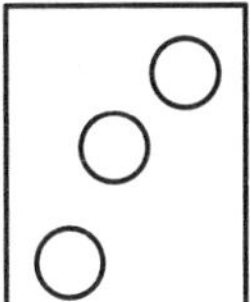

   ○   9 is 2 and 5 and 2.

   ○   6 is 3 and 3

   ○   9 is 4 and 4 and 1.

   ○   9 is 3 and 3 and 3.

Problem-Solving Strategy: Act It Out

Fill in the ○ for the correct answer.

---

1. 

Which time is 1 hour after 6 o'clock?

○ 5 o'clock   ○ 7 o'clock

○ 9 o'clock   ○ 4 o'clock

---

2. 

Which time is 2 hours after 8 o'clock?

○ 10 o'clock   ○ 7 o'clock

○ 6 o'clock   ○ 11 o'clock

---

3. 

Which time is 3 hours after 3 o'clock?

○ 12 o'clock   ○ 6 o'clock

○ 4 o'clock   ○ 2 o'clock

---

4. 

Which time is 1 hour after 11 o'clock?

○ 12 o'clock   ○ 4 o'clock

○ 2 o'clock   ○ 3 o'clock

Name _________________________________

Problem-Solving Strategy: Act It Out

Circle the correct letter for the answer.

1. Tori wants to buy a bag of pretzels from a vending machine that cost $0.70. If she has one quarter and the rest are dimes and nickels in her wallet, what are the least number of coins she can pay with?

   A 3   **C** 4
   B 5   **D** 6

2. Brenda has 13 animal crackers. Vince has 3 animal crackers. Brenda wants Vince to have the same number of animal crackers that she has. How many should she give him?

   A 3   **C** 4
   B 5   **D** 6

3. Judy has a square sheet of paper. How many times should she fold it to get 8 triangles that are all the same size?

   A 3
   B 5
   C 4
   D 6

4. What are the least number of straws you would need to make 6 congruent triangles? (Hint: 1 straw can form a side of two different triangles.)

   A 12   **C** 16
   B 18   **D** 24

5. Maggie and Seth look for fossils on a beach. In the morning they find 11 fossils. In the afternoon they find 6 more. Their father has 5 more for them. If they want to share the fossils, how many should each child get?

   A 4   **C** 6
   B 11   **D** 22

6. There are 21 children waiting in line to be admitted into a roller-skating rink. Olivia is seventh in line. How many more children are there behind her than in front of her?

   A 6   **C** 8
   B 7   **D** 14

Problem-Solving Strategy
Look for a Pattern

Fill in the ○ for the correct answer.

Use the table for Questions 1–2.

Number of Ducks	1	2	3
Number of Feet	2	4	6

1. How many feet do 3 ducks have?

   1 foot   6 feet   4 feet   8 feet
   ○   ○   ○   ○

2. How many ducks are there if there are 8 duck feet?

   2   4   6   8
   ○   ○   ○   ○

Use the table for Questions 3–4.

Number of Gloves	1	2	3	4	5
Number of Fingers	5	10		20	

3. How many fingers are there in 3 gloves?

   15 fingers   10 fingers   5 fingers   25 fingers
   ○   ○   ○   ○

4. How many fingers are there in 5 gloves?

   10 fingers   15 fingers   25 fingers   5 fingers
   ○   ○   ○   ○

Name ____

Problem-Solving Strategy: Look for a Pattern

Circle the correct letter for the answer.

1. What is the next figure in the pattern?

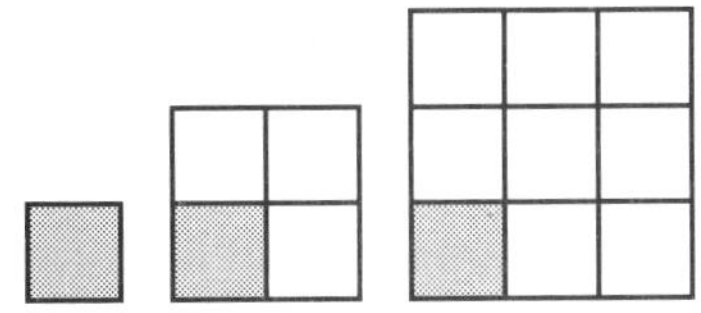

A 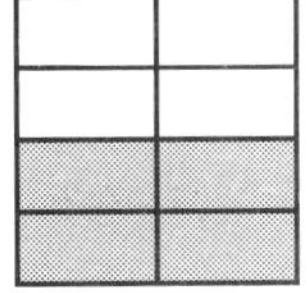   **C** 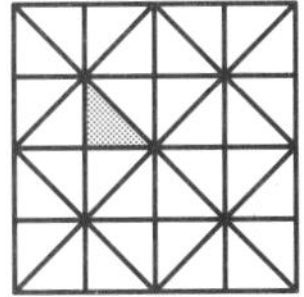

B 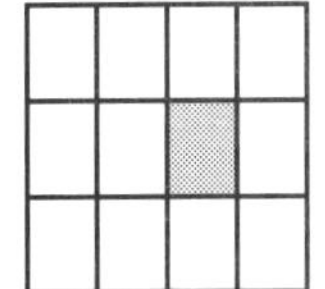   **D** 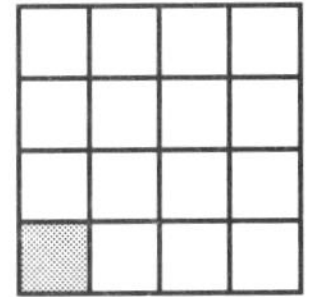

2. What is the next number in the pattern?

9, 12, 15, 18, 21, 24, …

A 25   **C** 27
B 29   **D** 32

3. Hobby's is having a grand opening and giving out prizes. The prizes will be given out according to a pattern. The store will give a prize to the 8th, 16th, 24th, and 30th customer who enters the store. Which customer will get the next prize?

A 32nd   **C** 38th
B 36th   **D** 40th

4. What is the pattern?

40, 36, 32, 28, 24, 20

A add 4
B subtract 4
C add 2 and subtract 1
D subtract 6

5. Each house on Tony's street has an odd number. If the first house is 211, what is the fourth house?

A 213   **C** 215
B 217   **D** 219

6. Which number would complete the pattern?

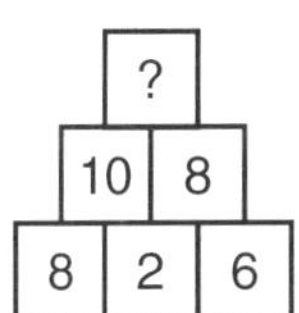

A 20   **C** 18
B 10   **D** 6

7. What is the next number in the pattern?

$$50 + 5 = 55$$
$$505 + 50 = 555$$
$$5{,}005 + 500 = 5{,}505$$

A 50,005 + 5,000
B 50,500 + 500
C 50,000 + 500
D 55,055 + 5,050

Problem-Solving Strategy
Try, Check, and Revise

Fill in the ○ for the correct answer.

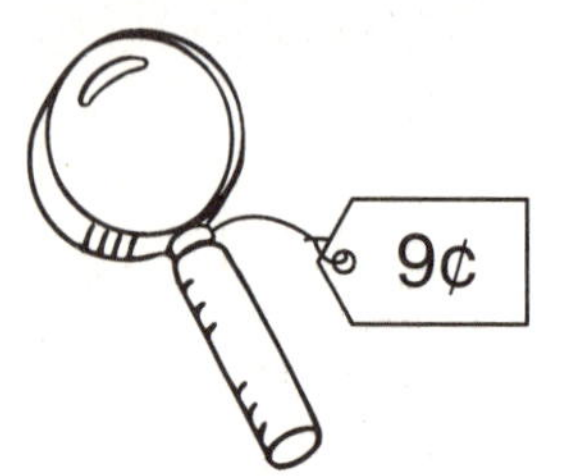 9¢   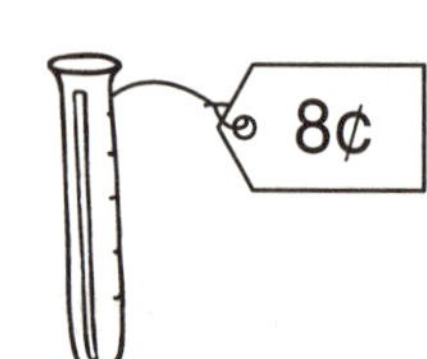 8¢   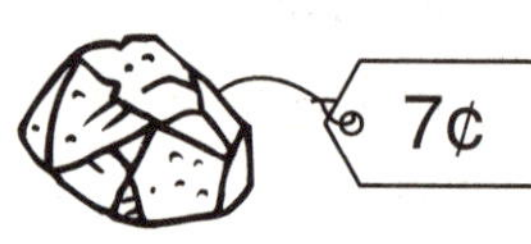 7¢   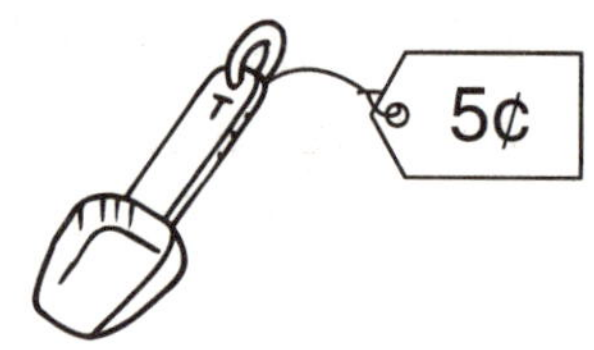 5¢

1. Which two items together cost 16¢?

○    ○    ○    ○ 

2. Which two items together cost 12¢?

○    ○    ○    ○ 

3. Which two items together cost 17¢?

○    ○    ○ 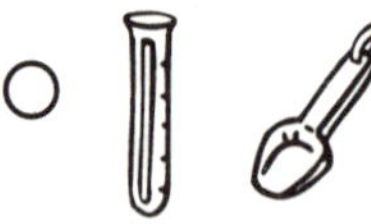   ○ 

4. Which two items together cost 13¢?

○    ○    ○    ○ 

5. Which two items together cost 14¢?

○    ○    ○    ○ 

Name ______________________________

Problem-Solving Skill: Try, Test, and Revise

Circle the correct letter for the answer.

1. Raul bought 1 football card and 1 baseball card. The football card cost twice as much as the baseball card. Raul spent $12. What was the cost of the baseball card?

   A $2   **C** $4
   B $6   **D** $8

2. Lisa has 15 bunnies in all. She has 3 more brown bunnies than gray bunnies. How many gray bunnies does she have?

   A 3   **C** 6
   B 9   **D** 11

3. Tony delivers pizza. In his money pouch are 8 bills worth $28. If he only has $1 and $5 bills, how many $5 bills does he have?

   A 2   **C** 3
   B 4   **D** 5

4. 2 adults and 3 children ride the bumper cars for $14. If the adult's fare is twice as much as the child's fare, what is the adult fare?

   A $1   **C** $2
   B $3   **D** $4

Use the information in the table for Questions 5–6.

Taylor Groceries	
Eggs	$1
Peanut Butter	$4
Sausage	$3
Cherry Pie	$6
Cheese	$2

5. Mollie bought 2 different items. She spent $8. Which items did she buy?

   A peanut butter and sausage
   B cherry pie and sausage
   C cheese and cherry pie
   D eggs and cherry pie

6. Christopher bought 3 different items and spent $9. Which items did he buy?

   A peanut butter, sausage, and cheese
   B cherry pie and sausage
   C eggs, peanut butter, and cheese
   D sausage, peanut butter, and eggs

7. Sally and her dad have a combined height of 108 inches. Sally is half the height of her dad. How tall is Sally?

   A 72 inches   **C** 40 inches
   B 54 inches   **D** 36 inches

Name _______________________________

Problem-Solving Strategy
Write a Number Sentence

Fill in the ○ for the correct answer.

---

1. Jess has 8 baseball cards and 4 basketball cards.
Which number sentence tells how many cards Jess has in all?

$8 - 4 = 4$	$8 + 4 = 12$	$4 + 4 = 8$	$8 + 8 = 16$
○	○	○	○

---

2. Marcia made 7 bracelets. She gave 3 bracelets to friends.
Which number sentence tells how many are left?

$7 + 3 = 10$	$3 + 3 = 6$	$7 - 3 = 4$	$12 - 7 = 5$
○	○	○	○

Use the table for Questions 3–4.

Players	Game 1	Game 2
Harvey	5	7
Juanita	8	4

3. How many points did Harvey score altogether in Games 1 and 2?

12 points	7 points	13 points	5 points
○	○	○	○

---

4. How many more points did Juanita score in Game 1 than Harvey?

5 points	12 points	8 points	3 points
○	○	○	○

Problem-Solving Strategy
Write a Number Sentence

Circle the correct letter for each answer.

1. Hazel is 52 inches tall. Her brother Francis is 37 inches tall. How many inches taller is Hazel than Francis?

   A 5   **C** 25

   B 15   **D** 89

2. One aquarium at the zoo has 9 fire salamanders and 3 tegu lizards. How many animals are in that aquarium?

   A 3   **C** 12

   B 16   **D** 27

3. A passenger van can seat 12 passengers. If 36 flute players need to be driven to a band concert, how many vans will be needed?

   A 432   **C** 3

   B 24   **D** 2

4. Muffins from Unlimited Bakery are packaged 6 in a box. John purchases 5 boxes for a meeting at work. How many muffins did he buy?

   A 1   **C** 30

   B 11   **D** 40

5. There are 8 players on Kasandra's soccer team and 2 more than that on Michael's team. How many players are on Michael's team?

   A 4   **C** 16

   B 10   **D** 18

6. On Tuesday the high temperature reached 78 degrees. On Wednesday the high temperature was 84 degrees. How many degrees warmer was Wednesday's high temperature?

   A 16   **C** 8

   B 12   **D** 6

7. Jennifer's mother cut 15 pieces of watermelon for a family picnic. At the end of the picnic, 7 pieces were left. How many pieces of watermelon had the family eaten?

   A 8   **C** 12

   B 9   **D** 22

Name ___________________________

Problem-Solving Strategy
Use Logical Reasoning

Fill in the ○ for the correct answer.

Which will you need most to measure each object?

1.

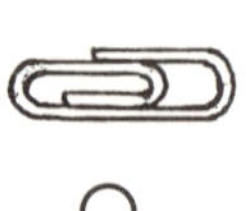　　○　　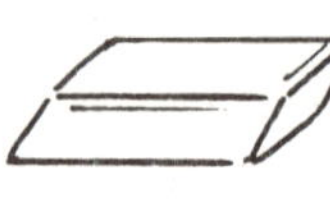　　○　　　　○　　　　○

2.

　　○　　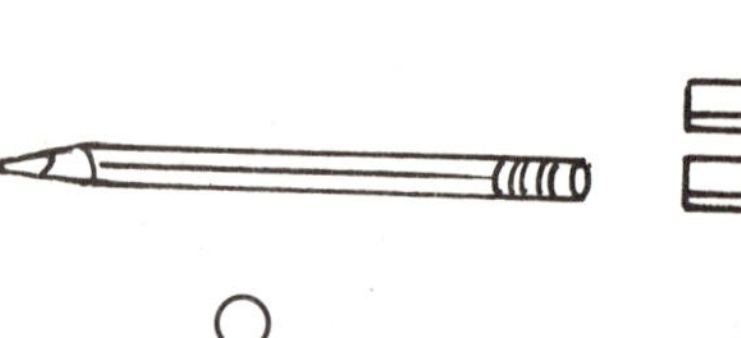　　○　　　　○

Which will you need fewest of to measure the object?

3.

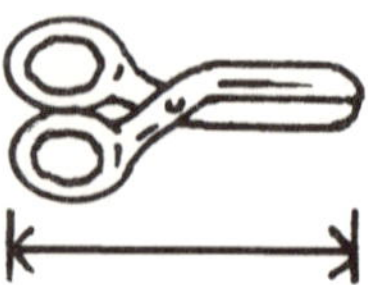

　　○　　　　○　　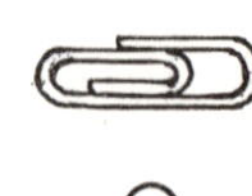　　○　　　　○

Name ____

Problem-Solving Skill: Use Logical Reasoning

Circle the correct letter for the answer.

1. Jerry is playing hide-and-seek with his little sister. She could hide in the bedroom, playroom, living room, kitchen, or bathroom. Use the clues below to find out what room she hid in. The room did not have a sink. People do not sleep here. There are no toys found in this room.

   A living room
   B kitchen
   C playroom
   D bedroom

2. Tina, Joe, Pam, Michelle, and Nan are in a race. Tina finishes first. Pam finishes before Nan and after Michelle. Joe finishes last. In what order did they finish the race?

   A Tina, Michelle, Nan, Pam, Joe
   B Tina, Nan, Michelle, Pam, Joe
   C Tina, Michelle, Pam, Nan, Joe
   D Tina, Pam, Michelle, Nan, Joe

3. Micah, Ric, Julio, and Cal are playing soccer. They have maroon, red, jade, and clear water bottles. Use the clues to determine what color water bottle Julio had.
   The color of Cal's water bottle began with the same letter as his name. The other boys did not. Ric's water bottle was hard to find because it blended in with the grass.

   A maroon   **C** red
   B jade   **D** clear

4. Simon is thinking of a number between 45 and 55. There is no 4 in the tens place. It is not divisible by 2. The sum of its digits is not 6.

   A 50   **C** 53
   B 51   **D** 54

5. The secret number is an odd number between 30 and 40. The sum of its digits is 10. What is the number?

   A 46   **C** 33
   B 38   **D** 37

Problem-Solving Skill: Solve a Simpler Problem

Circle the correct letter for the answer.

1. The Marker family is putting a fence around their garden to keep the rabbits out. The garden is square. If there will be 15 posts on each side of the garden, how many posts will they need altogether?

   A 64   **C** 54
   B 60   **D** 50

2. How many diagonals can be drawn in the figure shown?

   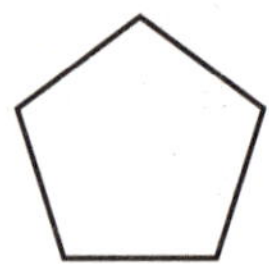

   A 5   **C** 14
   B 9   **D** 20

3. The cross-country ski trails at Oak Openings have signs posted every 300 yards. There is also a sign to mark the start of each trail. Alice starts on the red trail and has just passed the fourth sign. How far has she skied on the red trail?

   A 300 yards   **C** 1,500 yards
   B 900 yards   **D** 1,800 yards

4. Sammy and his friend Don are organizing the Boy Scout knot-tying contest. They have a piece of long rope that they need to cut into 20 pieces. How many cuts must they make?

   A 20   **C** 15
   B 19   **D** 10

5. Ryan numbered the note cards for his report, 1 through 25. How many digits did he write?

   A 10   **C** 41
   B 25   **D** 50

6. For an art project, Beth needs to cut strips of paper 4 inches long and 1 inch wide from a sheet of paper that is 8 inches long and 6 inches wide. How many strips can she cut?

   A 2   **C** 12
   B 10   **D** 48

Name ______________________________

Problem-Solving Strategy: Work Backward

Circle the correct letter for the answer.

1. On the way home from school, Thomas lost 5 marbles, then he gave 3 to Max. When he got home, he had 6 marbles. How many marbles did he have when he left school?

   A 16   **C** 12
   B 14   **D** 8

2. Tina needs to arrive at school at 7:35 A.M. It takes her 10 minutes to walk to school and 45 minutes to get ready in the morning. What is the latest time she can get up in the morning so that she arrives at school on time?

   A 7:00   **C** 6:40
   B 6:45   **D** 6:25

3. A box has red and blue marbles. You put in 4 red marbles. You take out 1 blue marble. There are 8 marbles at the end, and the probability of selecting blue was $\frac{3}{8}$. How many red marbles were in the box at the start?

   A 0   **C** 2
   B 1   **D** 3

4. At the Craft Barn, you purchased a set of acrylic paints for $6 and 2 identical paintbrushes. You spent a total of $14. What was the cost of 1 paintbrush?

   A $8   **C** $5
   B $6   **D** $4

5. Jim divides a bag of candy into 5 equal piles. He gives 4 of the piles to friends and keeps one for himself. He eats 7 pieces of candy and has 5 pieces remaining. How many pieces of candy were in the whole bag?

   A 60   **C** 36
   B 48   **D** 24

6. Lee takes 15 minutes to shower and dress, 10 minutes to eat breakfast, and 20 minutes to do his chores and walk to his bus stop. If the school bus picks him up at 7:40 A.M., what is the latest time Lee can get up in the morning?

   A 6:45   **C** 6:55
   B 6:50   **D** 7:00

123